Today's Homeowner®

Kitchen
REMODELING

PLANNING
AND RESOURCE
GUIDE

CREATIVE
PUBLISHING
international

Credits

Copyright © 2000 Creative Publishing international, Inc. and Times Mirror Magazines, Inc.

Creative Publishing international, Inc.
5900 Green Oak Drive
Minnetonka, MN 55343
1-800-328-3895

President/CEO: David D. Murphy
Vice President/Editor-in-Chief: Patricia K. Jacobsen
Vice President/Retail Sales & Marketing: Richard M. Miller

Executive Editor: Bryan Trandem
Associate Creative Director: Tim Himsel
Managing Editor: Michelle Skudlarek
Editorial Director: Jerri Farris

Lead Editor: Phil Schmidt
Editor: Rose Brandt
Copy Editor: Tracy Stanley
Art Director: Kari Johnston
Mac Design Manager: Jon Simpson
Assisting Project Managers: Julie Caruso, Tracy Stanley
Photo Researchers: Angela Hartwell, Julie Caruso
Illustrator: Richard Stromwell
Manager, Production Services: Kim Gerber
Production Manager: Stasia Dorn
Production Staff: Laura Hokkanen

Today's Homeowner.

VP/Editor-in-Chief: Paul Spring
Executive Editor: Fran J. Donegan
Managing Editor: Steven H. Saltzman
Art Director: Sue Ng
Senior Editors: Leslie Plummer Clagett, Lynn Ocone, Joseph Truini, Joe Hurst-Wajszczuk

VP/Publisher: John W. Young
General Manager: Jill Raufman
President, Today's Homeowner: Jason E. Klein

Library of Congress
Cataloging-in-Publication Data

Kitchen remodeling: planning and resource guide
    p.   cm.
  At head of title: Today's homeowner.
  Includes index.
  ISBN 0-86573-589-1 (hard cover)--ISBN 0-86573-588-3 (soft cover)
  1. Kitchens--Remodeling. 2. Interior decoration. I. Creative Publishing
International.

TH4816.3.K58212 2000
6434.7--dc21
99-087082

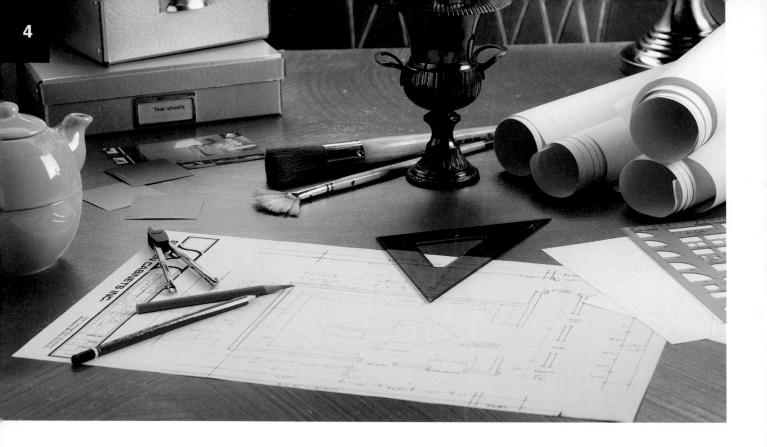

INTRODUCTION

It's a common experience: You're at a party; the hosts have carefully cleaned and prepared their entire house to accommodate guests, but before long, virtually everyone is crammed into the kitchen. What is it (aside from food) that draws people toward the kitchen? Maybe it's the bright, warm lighting or the cool, smooth surfaces, or the appeal of the space. Whatever the reasons, many people feel the kitchen is where they are really "at home."

Of course, how well a kitchen works is just as important as how it feels. Considering the vital role the kitchen has in every household and the constant use it gets, it's no mystery that kitchen remodels are among the most popular home improvements. What can be mysterious is the actual remodeling process—and that's where this book can help.

As a planning and resource guide, this book combines a thorough overview of each major step of the remodeling process with

an up-to-date resource guide featuring a wide range of products and information on where to find them. Whether you want to do-it-yourself, buy-it-yourself (and have someone else do the work) or hire a general contractor to do everything but cook the first meal in your new kitchen, this book offers creative solutions, current information and professional advice that will help you get the most out of the time and money you invest in remodeling your kitchen.

This book is divided into two parts. Part I: *Kitchen Planning*, walks you through the entire remodeling process, from the early stages of dreaming up your new kitchen to the closing days of the project. Each chapter covers a major step. To get you started, Chapter 1, *Exploring Your Options*, opens your mind to a world of possibilities and shows you clever ways other homeowners have used products and design ideas to get the most from their kitchens.

The remaining chapters in Part I are

devoted to helping you plan and complete the project, be it a simple cosmetic make-over or a major renovation job. You'll also learn where to find help when you need it. For example, many homeowners hire a kitchen designer to help with their remodeling project. The first part of this book will help you decide how much assistance you'll need and which professionals offer the services that best meet those needs.

As you read through Part I, you'll find periodic references to the worksheets found near the back of the book. These worksheets provide a place to keep track of the many details associated with your project and give you models for some of the legal documents you'll need when working with remodeling professionals.

While much of Part I includes step-by-step instructions to guide you through various stages of the remodeling process, it's best to read through the entire section before starting on your project. This can help you make some important decisions, such as when to hire professionals or when to schedule the project, before you spend a lot of time working out the details.

The second part of the book, Part II: *Kitchen Elements*, is a buyer's guide to all the major purchases typically involved in a kitchen remodeling project: cabinets, countertops, sinks, appliances, wall and ceiling finishes, flooring, lighting, windows and skylights. Each chapter provides an overview of your options, from old standards to products using the latest technology. You'll also find sound advice on the pros and cons of these products, to help you decide which are best for your kitchen and your lifestyle.

For each of these major components, there's a list of manufacturers who produce the products described. Most of the listings include web site addresses, so you can view the latest product lines and find dealers in your area from the comfort of your home.

Remodeling a kitchen is largely a matter of making careful decisions about function, style and budget. Using this book as a guide, you'll take a close look at how you use your current kitchen every day and find solutions for making it more comfortable, efficient and, of course, attractive. But the decisions are up to you, and that's what makes remodeling such satisfying work.

PART 1: Kitchen Planning

EXPLORING YOUR OPTIONS

When envisioning your new kitchen, it's important to look beyond the current limitations of the room and explore designs and features that could help you solve problems with your present kitchen—or become the building blocks of a radically new environment.

Even if you decide to scale down later to fit your budget, it's a good idea to consider a wide range of options during the initial planning stages. This will ensure that you don't overlook any potential solutions, and it may give you ideas for less expensive ways to create the effects you're looking for.

This chapter showcases a range of popular kitchen design options, including eat-in kitchens, island kitchens and open-plan kitchens. You'll find creative ways to stretch the space of a small kitchen or customize a kitchen to fit the way you and your family live. The section on universal design discusses ways to adapt a kitchen to make it easier to use for cooks of any size, age and ability.

In addition to practical suggestions about how to integrate important features into your new kitchen, the following pages are filled with photographs of model kitchens and design tips that will help you find the best solutions for your home.

■ *Opposite: This elegant eat-in kitchen serves double duty as an entertainment area and family gathering place.* ■ *Above: A blackboard and snack table allow busy family members to eat on the run and still stay in touch one another.*

Eat-In Kitchens

These days, the formal dining room is often the loneliest room in the house. Instead of dining together, most families tend to pause for a quick bite in the kitchen. That's why adding or improving an eat-in kitchen tops most kitchen remodeling wish lists. An "EIK" is also a savvy investment, because it's considered a basic necessity by a growing number of home buyers.

Analyzing Your Needs

Eat-in kitchens can be designed in a wide range of configurations. A few fundamental questions can help you focus your planning process.

What Will Fit the Available Space?

You don't need a huge kitchen to have a comfortable eating area—just about any layout can accommodate some kind of eat-in option. A narrow galley kitchen could use a space-saving pull-out table. An L- or U-shaped kitchen may be right for a table-height peninsula. And a kitchen with an island may benefit from a breakfast bar.

Of course, if your remodeling plan includes extensive layout changes, you have more options. For example, a new window alcove might be a great spot for a banquette—a table with built-in bench seating.

When planning an eat-in area, remember that location is critical: make sure that the table, chairs and diners won't disrupt the work triangle (see page 41) or the traffic ways that connect the kitchen to other parts of the house. Also, make sure your everyday dishes, glasses and flatware are conveniently within reach.

Who Will Use the Space?

Consider both your family's current needs and any changes you anticipate down the road. If there might be a baby in the picture, allow enough space (at least 2×2 ft.) for a high chair next to the table. If you'll be hosting a troupe of teenagers, consider an open-ended counter that allows meals to be served and eaten on-the-fly. For a kitchen used by older folks, make sure the seating is stable and easily accessible (pass on the three-legged bar stools, for example).

How Will the Room Be Used?

Consider how the eating area will be used, and design it accordingly. If the dining surface will double as a food-

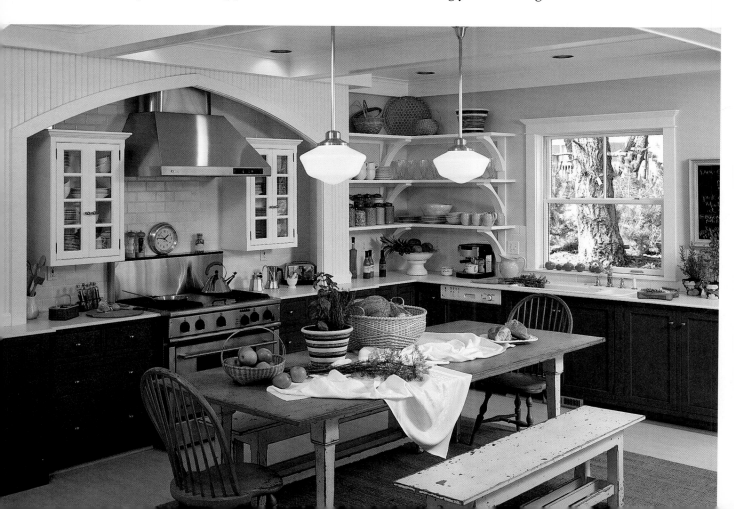

preparation center, choose a countertop of solid-surfacing rather than marble (which is vulnerable to knives, lemon juice, etc), or tile (which includes stain-prone grout). If it will double as a place to do homework or paperwork, choose an eye-friendly incandescent or halogen lamp instead of a fluorescent fixture.

Considering the Options

To find what might be right for your kitchen, consider the pros and cons of these popular eat-in configurations.

Freestanding Tables

The simplest eat-in kitchen option requires no construction, but it requires a lot of space. To seat four comfortably, you'll need a room that is a minimum of 220 sq. ft. Choose a 42-in. square or circular table or a 36×60-in. rectangular model, and allow an all-around clearance of 36 in., so that diners can push away from the table comfortably. If you need room to walk behind the chairs, increase this clearance to 65 in. If you select armchairs, be sure the arms will fit beneath the tabletop.

Table-height Counter Extensions

This option is as comfortable and convenient as a kitchen table, but it uses space more efficiently. You can create a table-height extension to a standard counter by dropping the surface height down to 30 in. For a support base, consider table legs, a pedestal or a trestle, and be sure to secure it to the floor for added stability. You can attach the counter to blocking inside an end cabinet or use brackets or cleats.

Breakfast Bars

A breakfast bar is a great option for a small household where informal meals are the norm. They're space-thrifty and can

■ *Opposite: Although a harvest table is a charming way to add an eating area to your kitchen, it does require a lot of space.*

■ *Above right: A table-height counter installed next to a base cabinet creates an unobtrusive, space-efficient eating area.*

■ *Right: This breakfast bar offers an informal dining surface as well as a serving counter.*

■ *Above: This Mission-style kitchen features a custom banquette that's surrounded by leaded-glass windows. The table, benches and cushions blend perfectly with the kitchen decor to create an elegant, functional room.*

■ *Left: A pullout table can be the ideal eat-in solution for a small kitchen. When not in use, this table slides into the base cabinets. And its proximity to the counters makes it a handy supplemental work surface.*

■ *Opposite: The table in this small kitchen provides a nice eating area for two without interfering with the main work areas. With the chairs pulled away, the solid-surface tabletop becomes a work surface suitable for many tasks.*

be a good way to screen kitchen clutter from view. However, this tall, narrow surface (usually 42 in. high) doesn't make a good work surface. And unless the bar includes a turn, diners must sit side-by-side. This may be fine for a couple, but it can become awkward for larger families. Allow a minimum of 24 in. per place setting—a three-place breakfast bar should be at least 6 ft. long. Select stools that have seats at least 30 to 32 in. high and have footrests to help prevent back strain.

Banquettes

Adding a built-in dining nook can be a great way to make your kitchen a more inviting place for meals and everyday lingering. Although they generally cost more than other kitchen dining options and may require a lot of space, banquettes have many advantages. The bench seating is fun for kids and offers a convenient way to bring the family together for meals. Benches built with flip-up seats are also great for storage. From a design standpoint, banquettes can unify adjoining spaces, an effect that's enhanced by coordinated bench cushions, window treatments and other decor.

Pullout Tables

One of the best options for a small kitchen is a pullout table. Many cabinet manufacturers offer pullout tables that hide behind false drawer fronts when not in use. The biggest problem with a pull-out unit can be finding a spot where it won't interfere with kitchen work. Also, bear in mind that although it's easy to slide the table back in after eating, you'll need to move the chairs back and forth each time you use the table.

Pole Tables

These contemporary-style systems consist of a vertical pole running from floor to ceiling and as many tabletop and shelf units as you'd like to add. The units can be moved up or down and rotated 360° around the pole for maximum space-efficiency and versatility. Some models offer units for lighting and supplemental counter space.

■ *This spacious island combines cutting surfaces, a cooktop and an eating area in one convenient location.*

Locating an Island

The traditional spot for a kitchen island is the middle of the room. A center island provides a focus and organizes the work flow, while providing accessible counter space from all directions. If you have an enclosed kitchen, this location is your only option; it's the only place the island won't block the work areas or interfere with traffic.

A perimeter island works well in an open or semi-open floor plan, where it can simultaneously connect spaces and separate them. In open or semi-open kitchens, especially those without windows, people tend to stand at the island facing the adjoining area. So, if you install a sink or cooktop on the island, orient it so you can face the "public" side of the space.

It's important to size the island in proportion to the kitchen. An island that's too large will crowd the space and form an obstacle to traffic. If an island is too small, it won't be useful when you need it. There isn't much point in building an island that's less than 2 × 3 ft., and one that's 4 ft. wide is even more useful. If your kitchen is smaller than 10½ × 12 ft., consider other options, such as a rolling work cart, rather than a built-in island.

Islands that have amenities, like sinks and cooktops, need to be larger than simple work-area islands. A cooktop island requires at least 9 in. of countertop in front and back of the cooktop and 15 in. on each side, so pot handles don't stick out into the walkways. The top of the island should have at least 36 in. of continuous space for each cook.

Although there are no set rules for the overall size of an island, there are some guidelines for the space around it. Start with the distance between the existing cabinets and the island. The work aisles should be 42 in. wide for one cook, and 48 in. wide if two cooks often work together. The main traffic path through the kitchen should be at least 48 in. wide. In addition, you'll need at

Island Kitchens

Although it's been said that no man is an island, many people want an island in their kitchen. In fact, surveys show that 80 percent of home buyers consider a kitchen island to be desirable or essential. Kitchen islands can range from simple work and storage stations to multi-tiered custom units that include a sink, a cooktop, an under-counter refrigerator and a surface that's extended into a breakfast bar or table-height peninsula.

From a design standpoint, an island can form the central focal point of a kitchen, making meal preparation more efficient and helping direct the flow of traffic. An island can also serve as a boundary of the kitchen area, allowing the cook to interact with guests in another room.

The key to designing an island kitchen you'll love (and can afford) is to figure out which options will be most useful. For around $600, you can get a serviceable, basic island built from stock kitchen cabinetry and finished with a laminate countertop. However, the price can easily climb into the thousands if you decide to include a sink or cooktop. Keep the project affordable by choosing materials wisely and incorporating only the features that you'll find most useful.

least 42 in. of clearance in front of the refrigerator, oven and dishwasher to avoid being pinned against the island when opening or closing the appliance doors.

Giving It Shape

Like an island's location, its shape is often determined by the surrounding area. In enclosed rooms, the basic rectangle is the most popular shape. In open layouts, angular islands—L, Y or V shapes—can act as boundaries to delineate the kitchen without closing it in. While these designs cost more to build, they offer more room for appliances, shelves, drawers, wine racks, towel bars, pullout bins and other amenities.

Although most kitchen islands are rectangular, you may want to experiment with other shapes to see if they would work better with the shape of your kitchen. Round, semicircular and even kidney-shaped islands can be very attractive, but be aware that they're tricky to design and expensive to build. If you do choose a curved design, consider using a rectangular base cabinet and getting creative with just the countertop—curved countertops are generally far less expensive than curved cabinets.

Finally, remember that you can use the space above the island, as long as you don't obstruct the sight lines with solid cabinets. Common overhead additions include pot racks, vent hoods and pendant lighting.

Once you have an idea of the size and shape that would work best, create an outline of the proposed island on the floor with strips of tape. (Painter's tape works best; it's wide and dark and peels up easily.) Leave the tape in place for a few days, shifting it around until

■ *You can even create a simple island with a sturdy piece of stand-alone furniture, if it fits the style of your kitchen.*

you recognize and resolve any traffic pattern problems.

Taking Form

An island is basically a countertop supported by cabinets. If you require a non-standard cabinet size, you may need a custom-built base, but otherwise you can economize by using stock cabinets. Cabinet manufacturers offer specialized units designed for islands, but you can adapt standard base units for that purpose, as well.

Island cabinets used to be carefully matched to the style and finish of the other kitchen cabinets, but today there's a growing trend to dress them up as distinct pieces of furniture, using moldings, trims, brackets and decorative feet. The idea is to make the island look like a one-of-a-kind piece.

Since all four sides of the island will be visible, buy cabinets that have finished sides, or face any unfinished surfaces with a matching plywood "skin"—a thin sheet of finished plywood.

Stock base cabinets come in 3-in. wide increments, starting at 9 in. You can mix and match the units to get the dimensions you're looking for, but installation will be easier if you select one or two larger units, rather than many smaller ones. Standard base cabinets are 24 in. deep, and you can install them back-to-back to create an island that's 48 in. deep. Other options include using deeper base cabinets or backing a standard base unit with a 12-in.-deep wall cabinet, for a 36-in. depth.

If the island will link the kitchen and the family room and you're planning to put cabinets or shelves on the family room side, be sure to take into account the dimensions of any electronic equipment that will go into the units.

Topping it Off

Although standard countertops are 36 in. high, that doesn't necessarily dictate the height of your island. For example, breakfast bars are typically 42 in. high, table-height counters are usually about 30 in. high and baking centers should be lowered to a level that's comfortable for the cook.

Consider the possibilities of an island that has more than one surface level. A breakfast bar or table-height extension on your island can double as an informal eating area and a serving counter. In addition to providing a place to eat the meal as well as cook it, a two-tier island can be a great way to screen off any cooking mess from adjacent rooms—the higher eating level hides the lower work level. For more information on breakfast bars and table-height extensions, see pages 10-13.

When it comes to countertop material for an island, most people choose to match the material used for the existing countertops in the room. However, this isn't always possible, or even desirable, if the surface is intended for a specific use. For example, marble is great for baking areas but is a poor choice for a cutting surface.

Putting it to Work

If you're adding a sink, cooktop or electrical outlet to the island, you'll need to consider your local building codes and what you're building on. If the floor lies over a concrete slab, plumbing and wiring will be difficult, at best. On the other hand, if there's a basement or crawlspace under the floor—particularly if the floor joists are running the "right" direction—you should have plenty of room to work.

Outlets

Wiring an island isn't difficult; you can usually tap an existing circuit to provide the power you need. The National Electrical Code requires at least one electrical outlet on islands, but you may want more, depending on the size of your island and whether it will have a cooktop and built-in appliances, such as an under-counter refrigerator. Although outlets can't be mounted directly onto the countertop, you can install them on the side of the cabinet or, on a two-level island, on the backsplash. Once you've sketched out your design, consult an electrician.

Sinks

Supplying hot and cold water to an island sink is easy. In most cases, you simply tap the water lines nearest the island and route extension lines up through the floor to supply the new fixture. If you have basic plumbing skills, you can do this yourself.

■ *In some kitchens the most efficient solution is an unconventional shape, such as this triangular island/breakfast bar.*

■ *Above: This multi-level island is designed to hide the food preparation area from guests in the adjoining dining area.*

■ *Right: When designing a kitchen island, take advantage of the opportunity to add more storage space, especially if your existing storage areas are full.*

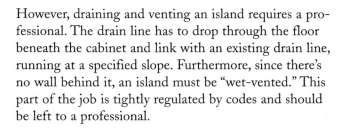

However, draining and venting an island requires a professional. The drain line has to drop through the floor beneath the cabinet and link with an existing drain line, running at a specified slope. Furthermore, since there's no wall behind it, an island must be "wet-vented." This part of the job is tightly regulated by codes and should be left to a professional.

Cooktops

Venting an island cooktop is usually more difficult than wiring it. One option is to suspend a vent hood from the ceiling and route the exhaust ducts to the outdoors. However, you'll need to conceal the ducting in a soffit or run it up through the roof. An island hood should be at least as wide as the cooking surface, but 3 in. wider on each side is even better. The height of the hood should be based on the manufacturer's recommendations; the standard height is 36 in. above the cooktop.

Another strategy is to select a cooktop that has an integral downdraft system or to mount an independent downdraft unit just beneath the cooktop. Both use powerful fans to draw fumes, moisture and odors through a surface-mounted grill, which directs them to ducts running beneath the floor, along joist spaces and through an outside wall.

Lighting

You won't be comfortable or safe working at your island if your hands are always in shadow. Lighting offers many opportunities to alter the appearance and functionality of your kitchen, so take your time choosing and placing the lighting fixtures. After all, the island is likely to become your family's favorite kitchen work area and gathering place.

Open-Plan Kitchens

If you're wondering how to make your small kitchen feel more expansive without adding on, consider the possibility of taking out a wall or two and converting the area to an open plan. While this option calls for careful planning, a building permit and some demolition work, it's quite feasible if you're planning a major kitchen remodel anyway—and the results will transform your home.

Planning to Expand

The first step is deciding which wall to remove. The best areas to combine with the kitchen are family and breakfast rooms, because this allows you to open up the space without changing the function of either room. Opening up a kitchen to a dining room is also an option, as long as you don't mind losing some of the formality of a separate dining room. However, avoid expanding into any room where privacy is important, such as a study or home office.

While they offer many advantages, open-plan kitchens often emphasize three problems that you'll need to consider in the planning stage: clutter, noise and odors.

Clutter

Open-plan kitchens put the cooking area in the spotlight. To keep it neat, make sure your plan includes ample storage space. If removing a wall means sacrificing some kitchen cabinets, add an island or peninsula with deep drawers and shelves, and use an appliance garage to reduce countertop clutter. Screen dirty dishes and cookware from view at mealtime with a change in the floor level or a multi-level peninsula or island.

Noise

Open kitchens allow noise to travel freely between rooms, which can pose a problem, especially when the kitchen opens to a family room. Since hard surfaces (like wood, tile and glass) reflect sound, use soft materials (like carpets, drapes and upholstery) wherever possible, to help muffle the sound of kitchen clatter, TV and video games.

Odors

The ventilation of your kitchen may be greatly improved by the new cross-breezes that appear when you remove a wall. However, the best insurance against the spread of cooking odors is good ventilation ducted through the roof or an exterior wall. Range hoods and downdraft vents are usually sized to fit a cooktop, but for an open kitchen you may want to choose one with a higher cfm (cubic feet per minute) rating.

Defining Space

An open-plan kitchen should feel expansive, not chaotic or formless. Fortunately, it isn't hard to define space without walls—in fact, there are many creative options. Using islands, peninsulas and furniture groupings are common ways to mark boundaries, as is the

■ *Adding a multi-level island is a popular way to separate the cooking and eating areas of an open plan. It can hide cooking messes, provide storage and serve as a buffet or staging area during meals.*

use of lighting. For example, you can adjust track lighting to outline an area. Architectural features, such as a picture window, fireplace, floor border (see **Designing with Flooring**, pages 120-121) or a transition in ceiling height can also provide borders or establish focal points for activity areas.

Although you may not need to move any of the activity areas after the walls come down, it's good to experiment with this to see how the new space will work best. For example, you might exchange the dining and sitting areas. When planning how to use the space, be sure not to intrude on the traffic paths; people need to move freely and efficiently through the rooms.

Another option that can enhance the usefulness of the open area is to add a nook or alcove somewhere. This space can serve as a cooking library, a craft center or simply as a quiet spot where you can sit down and pay bills, do homework or use the computer.

■ *One way to create an interesting boundary for the kitchen area is to design a peninsula that extends out into the open space.*

TIP

When the Walls Come Tumbling Down

Opening up a kitchen usually involves removing an interior wall. Although swinging a sledgehammer at a finished surface is a lot of fun, there are two things that you need to address before you get started. First, check for any plumbing, ductwork or wiring in the wall—if you find any, it needs to be disconnected, rerouted or capped before you start. Second, determine if the wall is load-bearing. If it isn't, you're almost ready to pick up the sledgehammer; if it is, you're in for a complicated process.

Load-bearing walls support the floors and roof of a house. If you remove a bearing wall without providing adequate support, you threaten the integrity of the entire house. All exterior walls are load-bearing, as are many lengthwise walls—and there can be others. How can you tell if a given

wall is load-bearing? It can be as easy as checking the attic to see if any joists, beams or rafters rest on the wall—or it can be far more complicated.

The bottom line is that this is *not* a learn-as-you-go project—if you can't rule out the possibility that it might be a load-bearing wall, you need to call in professional help.

Once the site is ready for demolition (with the utilities turned off, the heating and air-conditioning vents taped and the doorways sealed against dust) the contractor will strip away the drywall or plaster and support the ceiling joists on either side of the bearing wall with temporary walls. Then he or she will remove the wall and replace it as soon as possible with a permanent header and support posts.

■ *Left: An open plan, simple doors and clean styling make this 8 × 10-ft. kitchen appear larger.*

■ *Above: 42-in.-tall upper cabinets maximize storage without compromising valuable floor space.*

Small Kitchens

Whoever said "good things come in small packages" probably wasn't thinking about kitchens. If yours is 150 sq. ft. or less, it's "officially" small—and you're probably looking for ways to make it feel bigger and work better.

Fooling the Eye

When redoing a small kitchen, the primary visual goal is to make the room look bigger. To do this, use light finishes on all the surfaces, and keep the design and its details, such as the cabinet doors, simple. Use open shelves or glass doors with lighted interiors. To create a unified look, limit the number of textures and colors— white and one accent color are plenty. Subtle diagonal patterns make a room look bigger, and a mirrored backsplash can add the illusion of depth.

Good lighting is also essential. You can open up walls, add skylights or install bigger windows: clerestory windows placed high on the wall or large windows that run down to the counters work well.

Stretching Storage

The next most important goal usually is expanding storage space. Although it may be tempting, avoid putting cabinets on every wall; fewer cabinets make a room look bigger and give you more open space. For example, if you run cabinets along only one wall (a "Pullman kitchen"), you can extend the countertops into the corner and gain 24 in. of usable counter space.

Other storage ideas include extending cabinets all the way to the ceiling (use 42-in.-tall upper cabinets instead of 30-in. units) or using one tall pantry cabinet, or stacking two or three stock cabinets to create floor-to-ceiling storage. Stash a stepladder nearby, to help you reach the upper shelves. In any case, avoid the common mistake of suspending cabinets above a peninsula, where they block both light and conversation.

Store the items you use most at waist level, where they'll be easiest to access. To control clutter in the back of your shelves, add full-extension rollout slides—they're worth the extra cost.

While remodeling, consider creating shallow recessed

shelves in between the wall studs for storing small items, such as herbs, spices and canned goods. You can even build a recessed pantry between the studs and finish it to match your cabinetry.

Cabinet accessories, such as the rollout slides mentioned earlier, are great tools to help a small kitchen work smarter. Also consider a false sink front that stores sponges and cleaning items, or a multi-bin receptacle that hides trash and recycling in a base cabinet (see page 35). Use an 18-in.-wide drawer base that holds up to four bins.

Other cabinet accessories include: drawers in toekicks that hide lids and trays, shelving inside doors for storing spices and towels, vertical dividers that organize trays and cookie sheets, an under-cabinet rack for stemware, and a multi-level drawer divider for utensils.

Eating Efficiently

If you'd like to add an eating area to a small kitchen but don't know where to find the room, bear in mind that the least efficient spot for an eating area is the middle of the kitchen; there probably won't be enough room to walk around it. A small banquette or a table-height counter along a wall is a better choice. Other good options for small kitchens include pullout tables and pole tables (page 13).

Another space-saving idea is to double the function of the eating area. For example, a counter-height snack bar can also be used as a kitchen work surface. Choose a durable and appropriate material for these areas—perhaps butcher block, laminate or solid surfacing.

Rearranging Appliances

Now is the time to consider whether your appliances could be rearranged for greater efficiency. To do this, examine the way you use the appliances in your main work areas. Are the positions of the appliances causing you to waste time or effort as you cook or prepare food?

You can save cabinet space by ducting the range hood through a side wall, if possible, rather than up though a cabinet. A simple hood design, such as a stainless-steel model, usually looks best in a small space.

In a small kitchen, the location of the microwave can also pose a dilemma. If you put it over the range, you may have to reach over a hot surface to use it. Instead,

consider putting it next to the refrigerator, at eye level in a 12-in.-high wall cabinet. If you (or your children) can't reach it there, put it just below the counter.

If you're replacing any appliances, consider stretching your space by buying smaller units. A 27-in. oven, cooktop or range will leave you with 3 in. more countertop than a standard 30-in. unit—and the oven door will also require less room when open. You might also consider a 24-in. oven or an 18-in. under-sink dishwasher.

TIP

Claiming Corner Space

Corners are often key to stretching space and expanding a small kitchen. For example, consider eliminating the corner by placing something on the diagonal, such as a sink or a cooktop above an oven. If you need more wall storage, hang a lazy Susan cabinet over a corner sink. Or, you can install open-corner shelves that convert the corner into a display area, or add a corner window that provides light and a view.

■ *Kitchen corner cabinets can be inefficient, awkward and hard to access; instead, consider adding a sunny window.*

■ *Open racks under this cooktop provide efficient access to pots and pans, while extra-wide cabinet pulls make it easy to open the drawers, even with slippery fingers.*

rather cramped. Adapting your kitchen for more than one cook doesn't mean just adding more room; it means carefully examining the way you use the kitchen. The solution is to customize your kitchen to fit your family's budget, cooking habits and lifestyle.

Customizing the Layout

As with professionals' kitchens, a cook's kitchen should operate like an efficient production line. The goal is to organize the space so that cooking, cleanup and storage tasks can be done in sequence, with little wasted effort or doubling back. This can be done most effectively by creating distinct work zones for the major tasks. For example, you might set aside one "dry" area, for baking and dry storage and another area for "wet" tasks, such as filling stockpots or cleaning fish. While cleanup and wet prep can share one space, it's even better to have separate sinks. That way, one cook can rinse utensils and fill pots while the other can scrub and chop vegetables.

If you're modifying your kitchen layout, you can create a second work triangle (page 41) that shares one or two of the main triangle's "points," or work areas. In many two-cook kitchens, for example, the work triangles share the same cooking area and refrigerator. In others, they share only the refrigerator. Just make sure that the two triangles don't cross each other.

Buying Appliances

Not surprisingly, serious cooks tend to have a lot of cookware and crockery in a wide range of shapes and sizes. The dimensions of some specialty items can pose a problem: they won't fit on or in standard appliances. When shopping for appliances, be sure to bring a few of your largest pots, plates or platters to the showroom, just to make sure the models you're considering can accommodate them. (For more information on specific appliances, see **Appliances,** page101.) Here are some more buying tips to keep in mind:

Ranges & Cooktops

Because they offer instant heat and almost total control over heat adjustment, most serious cooks prefer gas burners for surface cooking. Today, there's a strong trend toward commercially adapted, or "professional-style," ranges and cooktops. These high-output gas appliances,

Kitchens for Cooks

Some families need only a basic kitchen, with enough cabinets, work space and appliances to prepare simple meals and clean up in time for the next round. But if you're serious about cooking, your remodeling project presents the opportunity to consider specialty appliances, fixtures, accessories and design elements that can make your kitchen a joy to use. A truly customized kitchen, with all the fancy features in just the right places, may be only a dream for most people, but the products and designs that go into pricey kitchens can generate useful ideas for every remodeling budget.

In today's two-career families, cooking has become a shared responsibility and an opportunity to bring the family together. However, since most kitchens were designed for just one cook, all this togetherness can get

modeled after units found in restaurant kitchens, have the proper size and safety features required for home use. But the race for the perfect cooking surface is still being run, and both gas and electric models have been improved to accommodate many specific cooking needs. Some key features to consider include:

• *Maximum and minimum output.* High-heat units boil water quickly, but not all burners are good for low-heat simmering.

• *Heat control.* Gas is generally still the best. However, some newer electric units use microprocessors to regulate temperature.

• *Burner size.* You may want a model that can heat oval pots or rectangular griddles.

• *Cleanability.* "Sealed" gas and glass-top burners are easier to clean than burners with catch pans.

Dishwashers

If your family produces a great deal of dirty dishes and pots, where you put your dishwasher might be more important than which brand you buy. This will depend on the layout of your kitchen, but the best spot is usually next to a sink.

As a general rule, select a dishwasher that provides the largest, most flexible interior space. Adjustable racks and fold-down tines help accommodate large and odd-shaped pieces. If you entertain frequently, you may want a model that has a custom cycle for fine china and glassware, as well as a pot-scrubbing cycle.

Also consider models that boost the water temperature above 120°F. These remove

grease and baked-on food well, and they allow you to keep your household water heater at a lower setting, which saves energy and reduces the risk of scalding.

Refrigerators

Select a refrigerator size and configuration that fits the way you cook and how often you shop. If you shop every day and don't need or want a huge refrigerator, select a smaller one that allows for more countertop space. You can always supplement it with a small bar refrigerator that will make ice and store a few frozen items. Multiple under-counter refrigerators, although costly, are another option for adding food storage space.

While you may like the look of built-in refrigerators, bear in mind that they are both costlier and shallower than freestanding refrigerators.

■ *Clearly, this kitchen was designed for a serious cook. The island features a cooktop and two built-in cutting boards. Both the refrigerator and the sink are within easy reach and traffic flows around the cooking area.*

Planning Storage

Since serious cooks often use a wide array of pots, tools and supplies, organization can be critical. To organize your cooking equipment, start by prioritizing it (not all of your cake pans are equally important). Put oversize items and those you use infrequently, like a turkey roaster, on a shelf in the basement. It's worth the occasional trip downstairs to get a seasonal item if it means more truly usable space for everyday things.

Before you finalize your kitchen layout, assess your storage needs. Measure and inventory everything you own, from your dinner plates to your largest tray, as well as any items you plan to buy.

If you're including distinct work zones in your kitchen, plan to store the appropriate equipment and supplies in their own zone. For example, stash measuring cups, mixing bowls, flours, sugar and spices in the baking area. If possible, each work area should have its own cutting board, knives, dish towels and other basic supplies handy, and don't forget a container for wooden spoons, spatulas and other tools. As a rule, store every item at its first point of use: keep the sauté pan near the range, and stow the pasta pots next to the sink.

■ *Converting a kitchen to fit two or more cooks typically means adding a food prep area; a second sink is also nice.*

Other ways to stretch your storage space include adding an under-cabinet pull-down holder for a cookbook or knife rack, a narrow under-cabinet shelf for spice jars and backsplash rails or hooks for hanging ladles and small pans.

Choosing Cabinets

Cabinets should be designed to take full advantage of options that help you save time and energy. For example, base cabinets with large, deep drawers instead of doors save you from having to get on the floor to retrieve items in the back of the cabinet. These drawers are ideal for storing almost anything—except pots, which should be stored on shallow shelves that pull forward in a base cabinet. Never store pots directly overhead; it's a safety hazard.

If the space is available, and you are installing custom or semi-custom cabinets, specify a 15-in.-deep upper cabinet in at least one spot, instead of the standard 12 in., to accommodate large serving dishes. And consider tall upper cabinets that extend up to the ceiling.

With cabinets of any size, adjustable shelves make it easy to customize your storage spaces. Avoid tiny knobs and hard-to-grasp decorative hardware. Instead, choose C- or U-shaped pulls that will allow you to open cabinets with one finger, even with gooey hands. Include a bank of 2- or 3-in.-deep drawers for small items, such as cookie cutters and custard cups, but be sure to get full-extension slides that allow the drawers to open all the way, so you can see items in back.

Choose closed cupboards (which hide clutter), and avoid open shelves (which gather dust). Remember that anything behind glass doors will be visible, so those are best for collections or decorative objects. And stay away from ornate grooves and molding details, which are hard to clean.

Adding Sinks & Faucets

The sink is the most-used work center in the kitchen. If there are two or more cooks in your household, you may want to include an additional sink in your plans. Even for one cook, a second prep sink is a nice luxury.

The primary sink should be roomy, making it easy to fill or wash large pots and serving pieces.

■ *Right: When you put a commercial refrigerator in a home setting, you usually need to cover it to suit the look of the kitchen. This refrigerator panel recalls the homey look of an antique tin pie safe.*

■ *Below: Well-organized storage is a critical element of a cook's kitchen. Keep tools and supplies, such as these spices and knives, next to their first point of use.*

Select the biggest sink you can accommodate, but don't exceed a depth of 9 in.; reaching down any farther can put extra strain on your back. And avoid rounded bowls and sinks that are divided into small double and triple bowls, as this reduces the size of your work area. An undermount sink is ideal for a busy cook, since you can wipe messes right into the sink bowl.

Faucets are available in an enormous range of styles, and you're likely to find just the right look for your kitchen. But before you go shopping, think about the faucet type that will function best. For example, single-handle lever faucets are much easier to operate than dial types: you can even use your elbow to flip them on or off when your hands are sticky or covered with flour. Gooseneck faucets make it easy to fill, wash and rinse large pots; a pullout faucet does the same, plus it allows you to reach all corners of the sink.

A useful specialty faucet is the pot filler—a cold water faucet usually installed on a wall near a cooktop or

range. This saves the cook from having to lug around big pots full of water, but for most people, it's a luxury.

Considering Surfaces

Kitchen surfaces, namely countertops and flooring, range from practical (laminate countertop, vinyl floor) to extravagant (copper countertop, terrazzo floor), and trends are always changing. But regardless of how much you want to spend and what look you're going for, remember that each surface material has positive and negative qualities for every application.

Since there's no countertop material that's perfect for all tasks, serious cooks often choose a variety of materials and place them to their best advantage: ceramic tile is highly resistant to heat—a good choice around a range or cooktop. Butcher block can be cut on without dulling knives, so it's great for prep areas. The smooth, cool surface of marble makes it ideal for rolling dough and candy-making. Your choices will depend largely on how and what you cook.

Placement of the countertop surface is also important for minimizing the inherent drawbacks of materials. Just to list a few: laminate is vulnerable to being scorched by hot pans or scratched by knives; concrete countertops, marble and ceramic tile grout are prone to staining; butcher block and other wood surfaces can warp and split and may harbor bacteria if not cleaned properly.

When it comes to kitchen flooring, three materials remain the most popular: vinyl, ceramic and wood.

■ *A butcher block surface is ideal for cutting and chopping but may suffer from water damage if installed near a sink.*

■ *This undermount sink has many handy features: a filtered-water tap, soap and hand lotion dispensers, a pullout faucet and a deep second compartment for washing vegetables.*

Specialty materials include cork, linoleum and epoxy surfaces. Since serious cooks spend a lot of time on their feet in the kitchen, comfort is an important consideration, along with washability, durability, slip resistance and, of course, appearance.

Vinyl is always a good choice: it's water-resistant, easy and clean and soft underfoot, although not as durable as some other types. Sheet vinyl in 12-ft.-wide rolls is best for kitchens because the floor will have fewer seams to catch dirt and water.

Ceramic tile is attractive and durable, and it's fairly stain resistant if you seal the grout periodically. But tile is a very hard surface, and it can be cold for bare feet (although some people solve the latter problem by installing in-floor heating).

Traditional hardwood strip flooring is another popular choice, but be aware that it's a high-maintenance product and is vulnerable to water damage. Other options include wood-and-plastic laminate flooring, which are better for replacement flooring than solid wood, because they're thinner and often can be installed over old flooring.

TIP

International Cooking

If you specialize in the food of a specific culture, a remodeling project is the perfect opportunity to adapt your kitchen to the cuisine of your choice. In addition to selecting the best materials and equipment for preparing traditional meals, consider adding some decorative elements that reflect the spirit and style of the culture.

MEXICAN COOKING

If you love Mexican cooking, aim for a warm, colorful space. For example, on the backsplash you might choose traditional Mexican tiles, and on the floors sun-baked saltillo tile (with the footprints of the chickens and cats that roam the yards where it's dried).

A specialized cooktop might include a commercial-strength gas burner for frying homemade tortilla chips, or a simmer burner (a full-sized burner that maintains low temperatures and prevents scorching) for cheese sauces and mole. Next to the cooktop, place a pantry filled with bins of baking essentials. Add a pullout tray to the pantry for bulk jars of your favorite spices.

FRENCH COOKING

Imagine your French kitchen centered around a large greenhouse window full of potted herbs. As for equipment, you could certainly make use of a double oven, with enough room to bake an entire meal plus a chocolate gateau. Add a rotisserie rack for meats and poultry and a terra cotta baking stone, to cover some of the basics. Make sure the cooktop burners offer plenty of power for searing meats, as well as consistent, low settings for simmering sauces. And don't forget to include a powerful food processor for puree.

A baking center would be perfect for pastries and bread. This could be an island built to just the right height or a lower section of counter that gives you extra leverage for rolling dough. You could also include a marble slab for making fondant and other confectionery.

ASIAN COOKING

There are many kinds of Asian cooking, and much of it is done in a wok. If you're an avid Asian cook, you might love having a wok room, a compact cooking space tailored to cooking with a wok. It should include a high-output gas burner, for quick-frying and immediate heat control; a powerful vent fan or vent hood, to exhaust the many strong odors and ever-present smoke produced by fry-cooking; and perhaps even a pot filler faucet, as a handy water supply for steaming. Although it's best to keep it small, a wok room should have space for cooking spices, oils and other ingredients and easy-to-clean counters.

To set the mood, consider an aquarium filled with vividly colored fish. Their gentle, rhythmic movements are calming and remind the cook that the essence of Asian cooking is harmony and balance.

User-Friendly Kitchens

One of the trends in kitchen design is a savvy combination of form and function called *universal design*. Born out of efforts to accommodate the disabled, universal design concepts are now applied to kitchens for all sorts of users—and it involves far more than simply lowering all the counters to wheelchair height. It means looking for ways to adapt the kitchen so that everyone in the family can use it comfortably. This might include lowering one counter and raising another so that users with different needs can prepare dinner together.

Another advantage of universal design is that you don't have to sacrifice style for comfort. In fact, it often gives a kitchen a custom-designed appearance. And in many cases, it doesn't require custom-made cabinets, as semi-custom cabinets now come with many of the options described below.

While you can add universal design elements to your kitchen at any time, significant changes, such as repositioning the cabinets or countertops, are best done during a full-scale remodeling project.

Providing Flexibility

The key to creating a kitchen that fits everyone in the household is flexibility. For example, adding a knee space under a sink or cooktop not only makes that area accessible to a person in a wheelchair, it allows someone else to sit on a stool while cooking or washing up, thus avoiding fatigue and back strain. A knee space can also provide a spot for a serving cart, which offers a lowered work surface and a way to set or clear a table in one trip.

Customizing the height of countertops and work surfaces is critical to ensure that kitchen tasks can be done comfortably and efficiently. One way to allow different people to work effectively together in a kitchen is to provide a customized counter height for each person.

To determine the right height, get into a comfortable working position at a low surface, such as a table. Gradually increase the height of the surface by stacking up boards or strips of plywood until you can rest your palms on the surface with a slight break in your elbows. Clamp the wood in place and complete a range of typical tasks, such as chopping, mixing and stirring, to make sure the height is right.

Once you've found the most comfortable level, plan to include a working surface at that height in your kitchen. You can invest in new counters, or use one of these tricks: To create a lower work surface, secure a cutting board over an open drawer. To raise a work surface, place a thick piece of butcher block on the counter. Other solutions include roll-out carts or heavy-duty full-extension shelves.

Using the Reach Zone

The placement of storage areas is another important element of universal design. The most comfortable "reach zone" is between the waist and shoulders, and up to an arm's length away. Unfortunately, many kitchens offer little or no storage in this zone, devoting the space instead to countertops.

To add more reachable storage, consider adding pantry cabinets or a stand-alone

■ *This universally designed kitchen with KraftMaid® cabinets features a raised dishwasher cabinet, lowered countertops and extra-high toekicks.*

■ *Create a lowered counter with heavy-duty full-extension drawer slides that telescope out to provide a sturdy surface.*

pantry unit to your kitchen. Another option is to place shallow storage shelves at the back of the countertops.

Making It Easy on the Eyes

Poor lighting is one of the most common culprits in inefficient kitchens. Most kitchens have good ambient light, but not enough task lighting, which leads to eye strain and fatigue. The solution is to install under-cabinet task lighting that brightens the major work areas (see **Kitchen Lighting**, pages 132-135).

To make it easier to find your way around the kitchen in dim light (such as on a midnight snack run), you can add a contrasting edge molding around the countertop or a contrasting border on the flooring.

Even if the lighting in your kitchen is adequate, if there are intricate patterns on the countertops or the flooring it can be difficult to find dropped items. Subtle patterns and neutral colors are most practical.

Adding Accessibility

To turn your kitchen into a work space everyone in your household can move around in and use more comfortably, begin by considering some of the ideas listed below:

Cabinets & Drawers

• Hang some of the wall cabinets low so the shelves will be easy to reach. Leave some cabinets at standard height to keep them from looming over the counters.

• Install base cabinets with removable or slide-away doors to create a knee space; patch or extend the flooring to the back of cabinet to provide an even surface for wheelchairs or stool legs.

• Add large drawers in the base cabinets to provide easy access to pots and other everyday items.

• Replace stationary shelves with pullout shelves.

• Use quality full-extension slides on drawers and pullout shelves for safe, reliable operation.

• Put lazy Susans in all corner cabinets.

• Add open shelves under wall cabinets, or hang small pots and pans from hooks.

• Replace cabinet knobs with easy-to-grasp pulls.

• Add extra-high toekicks to allow wheelchair access and to raise the bottom shelves and drawers.

Counters

• Provide a range of flexible or customized countertops at a comfortable height for each person who uses the kitchen.

• Install a fold-down counter surface that can act as a work surface, eating bar or desk space.

• Add a contrasting countertop edge molding with rounded corners; it will be safe and easy to see in the dark.

Sinks & Faucets

• Replace a two-knob faucet with a single-lever pullout faucet.

• Add a knee space under a sink by plumbing the drain of the sink in back and placing a removable panel over the pipes.

• Place the sink and cooktop near each other and at the same level, to make it easy to move pots back and forth.

Appliances

• Select a side-by-side refrigerator/freezer, which offers storage at all levels.

• Raise the dishwasher so that it can be loaded and unloaded with less bending.

• Consider a range or cooktop with touch-sensitive controls, which are easier to use than traditional knobs.

ASSESSING YOUR NEEDS

As you looked at the wonderful photographs and considered the many ideas offered in the first chapter of this book, you were probably thinking of what "might be." Now it's time to take a close look at "what is."

The goal of this step is get some idea of how big your remodeling project will be. Will you choose a simple cosmetic makeover or splurge on a major room addition? You can change your mind later, of course, (and financial realities may change it for you), but now is the time to decide what works and what doesn't and to think about what would be involved in remodeling your kitchen.

It all starts with a careful examination of the ways in which you use your kitchen—for everything from midnight snacks to holiday dinner parties. In the process, you'll spend some time taking notes and even some measurements, and you'll make a list of the problem areas as well as positive aspects of your current layout.

After you've made some initial assessments, take a look at **The Five Levels of Kitchen Remodeling** (pages 36-37), to see what category your combined needs and wishes fall into. This can help define the project as a whole and give you a sense of how much help you'll want or need to finish the job. You'll also find it helpful to fill out **Worksheet 1** (pages 146-147), which can serve as a reminder of some of the decisions you've made.

■ *Opposite: The owners of this "cook's kitchen" clearly focused on plentiful natural lighting and an open, airy feel. They also included ample counter space near the major work areas.* ■ *Above: More than food preparation takes place in the kitchen. Here, a play area was set aside for small children.*

A Kitchen That Fits

Like your car or your clothing, your kitchen should fit and serve you well. In addition to accommodating the way you cook, eat and store food, it must harmonize with your home's design scheme and provide a comfortable gathering place for your family and friends.

How do you begin planning a kitchen that will do all that? Start with your primary motive for remodeling. Most likely it will focus on one of two issues: efficiency or appearance. In other words, your current kitchen may not work well for you, or it may just look outdated.

Taking Notes

Begin by taking a week or two to observe how you use your kitchen. Keep a note pad handy, and jot down any problems or annoyances that keep you from being efficient or comfortable when using the kitchen, as well as anything in the room that you find unattractive. Also note those elements that work well or aspects of the kitchen that you enjoy.

Imagine the way you perform daily tasks. Where do you set down the grocery bags when you come through the door? Is it convenient to unload the dishwasher? Where do you stack the dirty dishes as you cook? How easily can you slip away from the dinner table to check on something in the oven? What sorts of items do you leave out on the counters, and is there a better place for them? Where do people sit or stand as they chat with the cook?

Once you've documented the positives and negatives, start dreaming up possible changes. Refer back to the last chapter to help develop your ideas. You can learn more about specific products and materials in Part II of this book. Also, talk to friends about what they like and dislike about their own kitchens.

Don't worry about the cost yet. There will be plenty of time to bring your fantasies down to earth as you move through other planning stages. At this point in the process, the key is to consider every possibility.

Fulfilling your kitchen fantasy may be as simple as installing pantry shelves in your cabinets, or as dramatic as adding a glassed-in sunroom. When adapting a kitchen to your needs, think in broad terms about the issues at hand.

If you've lived with a small kitchen for years, you may think of the room simply as a place in which to prepare and store food and clean up after meals. As you brainstorm your kitchen, remember that this room can serve many other functions, as well. If your kitchen has no eating area, consider adding a breakfast nook. If your home doesn't have a den or study, you might include an office space or a study desk.

Also consider how your household will change over the next fifteen years. The needs of a family with young children who will soon become teenagers are quite different than the needs of a mature family whose children will soon leave for college.

■ *Consider how your kitchen could best fit your lifestyle; you might include casual office space for everyday tasks.*

Looking at the Layout

Kitchen remodeling projects can be grouped into five levels, based on how much the room's layout will be changed (there's more information on each level at the end of the chapter). To determine the amount of change you need, ask yourself a few questions. Do you have enough space to prepare meals? How far apart are the refrigerator, range and sink from one another? Are there efficient and convenient pathways through the kitchen—or are other people always crossing your path as you work? Is there an adequate eating area; does the eating area block the flow of traffic through the room?

If you've identified problems with your layout or floor plan, ask yourself if they can be corrected simply by rearranging your existing kitchen. If not, explore how you might address them, perhaps by adding or moving doors, redirecting traffic or expanding the kitchen.

If your current needs are few, or you simply want a new look in your kitchen, you'll probably plan a Level 1 project—a relatively inexpensive cosmetic makeover, in which you simply redo the surfaces and make no (or very minor) changes to the layout and floor plan. This level of project is popular because the cost is relatively low and many homeowners can complete most of the work themselves.

If, on the other hand, you'd like to move the refrigerator over a few feet or put the sink closer to the range, you're probably thinking about a Level 2 project; with a Level 3, you're likely to rearrange the whole kitchen. A Level 4 often means knocking out an interior wall to expand the kitchen into adjacent an room, while a Level 5 involves an expansion that requires a room addition. With each higher level, you're likely to need more professional help, but even a Level 5 job offers several tasks you might choose to do yourself, including managing the job.

Reviewing the Elements

The following is an overview of the major kitchen elements. As you assess your needs and desires for each, use **Worksheet 1** (pages 146-147) to record your thoughts.

Countertops & Work Areas

Countertops are one of the most important visual elements of a kitchen, and replacing them is a common kitchen remodeling project. Since a kitchen is first and

■ *The cabinets and countertops you choose will largely determine the look of your new kitchen. For a cozy feeling, choose rich, warm colors; for a more open feeling, choose light colors.*

foremost a place to prepare meals, almost any kitchen can be improved by adding more countertop space. An outdated, worn or unattractive surface is also a perfectly good reason to redo your counters. A beautiful new countertop can not only transform the look of your kitchen, but increase the resale value of your home, as well.

■ *This cutting board fits over a drawer to provide additional work space next to the range.*

When evaluating your countertops and work areas, ask yourself the following questions: Is there enough space to perform kitchen tasks? Are two or more people able to work at the same time without bumping into one another? Is there enough countertop work space around the sink, cooktop, oven and refrigerator? Is there at least one long, uninterrupted countertop where you can assemble meals and prepare recipes? Or, do you have the rarer problem of too much counter space, so that the sink, stove and refrigerator are too far apart to use efficiently?

■ *A well-planned kitchen will have good background lighting, generous task lighting over work areas and accent lighting to highlight decorative features.*

If you determine that you don't have enough counter space in the right locations, ask yourself if the problem can be remedied with a Level 2 or a Level 3 rearrangement. If not, or if you clearly don't have enough room to work, consider adding to the size of your kitchen with a Level 4 or Level 5 expansion.

In some cases, the problem isn't really a lack of counter space; it's a lack of storage space that results in cluttered counters. If small appliances are taking up too much workspace on your countertops, consider installing a cabinet that's specially designed to store these items.

Cabinets & Storage

Adding, replacing or resurfacing kitchen cabinets is another relatively simple way to make a kitchen look brand new. To assess the changes your cabinets might need, ask yourself: Does the kitchen have adequate storage space for all the food, dishes and utensils? Are the food, tools and equipment stored near their points of first use? Are the frequently used items stored within easy reach, 2½ to 5 ft. above the floor? Also, is all of the space, including the corners and the spaces above appliances, being used well?

If there are problems with your existing cabinets, determine if you can solve them by organizing the cabinets more efficiently, or by adding features such as a lazy Susan and slide-out shelves. If not, you may need to redesign your cabinetry or expand your kitchen to add more storage space. If you have more cabinet space than you need, consider replacing some cabinets with a countertop desk area or a built-in appliance, such as a microwave oven.

Electrical & Lighting

Do you blow a fuse or trip a circuit breaker every time you turn on the toaster and the coffee maker at the same time? If you have a typical older kitchen, you probably don't have enough amperage or electrical circuits to power all your appliances—and a remodeling project is the ideal time to address this problem.

Another common problem is insufficient lighting, especially task lighting for work areas. Without it, you're typically working in your own shadow. Poor task lighting can be improved by adding recessed ceiling lights, track lighting or under-cabinet light fixtures. Poor background lighting can be remedied by adding light fixtures, skylights or windows.

Another lighting project that can dramatically improve the appearance of a kitchen is simply replacing outdated lighting fixtures with new ones. In most cases, this is a small job that doesn't require extensive rewiring.

Appliances & Plumbing Fixtures

Think about your major appliances and plumbing fixtures. Are any of them more than fifteen years old? If so, they're probably at the end of their useful lives and should be replaced during your remodeling project.

Even if your appliances aren't old, it may still be worthwhile to upgrade them. During your planning process, research current models to determine if an investment in more energy-efficient appliances would save you money in the long run. Common plumbing and appliance improvements include upgrading faucets, adding a water purifier and replacing a countertop microwave with a model that fits into a custom cabinet.

Many homeowners replace plumbing fixtures and appliances simply for cosmetic reasons. However, if you have an energy-efficient, high-quality appliance that's only a few years old, you might consider simply refinishing it to match your new decorating scheme.

In addition to upgrading your major appliances, consider adding some of the many useful small appliances that are available, such as trash compactors, warming drawers, instant hot-water taps, cabinet-mounted can openers and built-in stereo and television units.

Floors, Walls & Ceilings

Your kitchen floor, walls and ceiling provide the backdrop for all the other elements of the room—and if you plan to add beautiful new appliances, counters or cabinets, it's almost always worthwhile to make sure the old surfaces won't suffer in comparison. You may want to replace the old surface coverings or simply renew them—a relatively easy and inexpensive option. Either way, you're sure to feel that the investment was well worth it when you see the impact the change has on the room.

Installing new flooring is an excellent way to transform a kitchen, since it's usually the largest surface in the room. Redoing the wall

surfaces typically involves repainting or hanging new wallpaper. However, if you're adding or moving walls, you'll have additional decisions to make in order to match existing walls.

Kitchen ceilings are generally given a fresh coat of paint whenever the walls are refinished, but you can also consider a beadboard paneled ceiling, a tin ceiling or a bold texture.

■ *Left: If your current sink is too small, a new sink and plumbing fixtures can transform your feelings about kitchen cleanup chores.*

■ *Above: When planning your new cabinetry, be sure to include a convenient place to deal with trash and recycling containers.*

TIP

Planning to Sell

If your remodeling goal is simply to improve the value of your home in preparation for selling it, consider the following advice from real estate agents.

In general, it isn't a good idea to put in a luxury kitchen if you plan to sell the house in the near future; it will be difficult to recoup your investment in top-of-the-line appliances, cabinets and countertops. Instead, make sure your kitchen layout is sound, and replace any aging materials with good-quality, medium-priced products in a neutral, light color scheme. For example,

rather than installing an integral solid-surface sink and countertop, select a stainless steel sink and a laminate countertop. Instead of a tile or solid wood floor, select good-quality vinyl sheet flooring.

Although a wisely planned kitchen remodel can pay for itself in home equity, real estate values vary widely and are affected by many factors. If you plan to sell your home, consult an experienced real estate agent before starting your project, to find out how much a remodeled kitchen would actually be worth in your case.

The Five Levels of Kitchen Remodeling

Your kitchen remodel will probably fall into one of these five categories, based on the overall objective of the project. A Level 1 project is aimed at making your kitchen look better, although a new countertop and new flooring may make it easier to use, too. At the other end of the range, a Level 5 project will completely change your current kitchen, as well as enhance the exterior design of your home.

The typical costs given for each level are merely averages, and your project expenses may vary widely from these. Determining the level of project required to meet your needs can be a lengthy process involving many factors. For more help with estimating costs and setting a budget for your remodel, turn to **Finding the Financing,** page 49.

■ *Top: The kitchen before a Level 1 remodel.* ■ *Above: After the cosmetic makeover, the kitchen has a fresh new look, and the addition of a base cabinet provides useful countertop space next to the range.*

Level 1: Redoing the Surfaces

The most basic level of remodeling is the cosmetic makeover, in which you leave the layout unchanged and simply redo the surfaces. Typically this involves renewing the walls, floors, cabinets and countertops, while retaining many of the existing appliances and fixtures. Much of the work involved at this level will fall within the range of an experienced do-it-yourselfer, although there are some exceptions, such as installing countertops and refinishing appliances.

At first glance, the kitchen shown here looks completely new—but looks are deceiving. The only layout change is the small base cabinet added in the corner next to the range. The new-looking appliances were simply refinished, and the cabinets were repainted and spruced up with new hardware. The biggest expense here was replacing the laminate countertop and backsplash with solid surfacing. In addition, the windows were retrimmed, the walls, flooring and ceiling surfaces were redone and recessed task lighting was added to illuminate the sink and countertop work areas. Typical cost: $2,000 to $7,000.

Level 2: Changing the Layout:

With this option, you'll retain the same basic footprint as the existing kitchen, but change the positions of the appliances, fixtures and eating areas to create a more efficient layout. This level of remodeling includes most elements of the cosmetic makeover, but may also require the work of a carpenter, electrician and plumber. Homeowners with advanced do-it-yourself experience might choose to do most of this work themselves. Typical cost: $5,000 to $15,000.

Level 3: Redirecting Traffic

In a slightly more complex scenario, you might find it necessary to change the layout more radically in order to redirect traffic moving through the kitchen. Often this means adding or moving a doorway in a partition wall, as well as redesigning the basic kitchen footprint. Unless you are a very experienced do-it-yourselfer, much of this work will require the help of subcontractors. At this fairly extensive level of remodeling, many homeowners also take the opportunity to add new windows, patio doors and skylights. Typical cost: $12,000 to $30,000.

Level 4: Expanding Within

If your present kitchen just isn't large enough to accommodate your needs, one option is to extend the room by borrowing space from adjacent rooms. This generally means that interior partition walls will need to be removed or moved, which is work for an experienced carpenter. This level of remodeling often includes significant rearrangement of the appliances and cabinets, as well as the installation of new windows, doors or skylights. In a major remodeling project of this kind, most of the work will be done by contractors, but many homeowners are capable of supervising the project. Typical cost: $20,000 to $40,000.

Level 5: Expanding Outward

If you find that more space is essential and you can't expand into adjoining rooms, then the remaining option is to build an addition onto your home. This ambitious undertaking requires the aid of virtually the same collection of professionals it takes to build a home from scratch: architects and engineers, excavation and concrete contractors, construction and finish carpenters, plumbers and electricians. At this level, most homeowners choose to hire a general contractor to manage the project. Typical cost: $30,000 and up.

WORKING WITH DRAWINGS

Now that you've made some decisions about the scale of your kitchen project, you can put your ideas on paper. Whether you're planning a cosmetic makeover or dreaming about an addition, drawings let you experiment with different layouts and force you to get down to the details of how the pieces of the project all fit together. Drawings also help as you select cabinets, appliances and fixtures; and they form the basis of the agreement between you and the tradespeople or contractor you hire.

If your remodeling project is big enough to require building permits, you'll need detailed architectural plans, or *blueprints*, to submit to the local building department; you or your contractor can have these drawn by an architect, draftsperson or qualified kitchen designer (see page 60), and some contractors draw plans, as well. But your own plans can have as little or as much detail as you'd like. This chapter shows you how to put together the basics—floor plan and elevations. **Worksheet 2** (pages 148 to 149) will introduce you to some standard drafting symbols used for drawing kitchen elements.

Before you get started drawing, review the kitchen design standards given on pages 41-42. These unofficial recommendations, developed over time by kitchen designers and other remodeling professionals, can help ensure your kitchen is comfortable and easy to use. Also keep in mind that there are many building codes and regulations that must be followed. Those given here are merely some guidelines; there are likely many more specific regulations that apply to your community and your project. Still, knowing some of the basic guidelines and building requirements can help you narrow your options. You may decide not to move a sink, for example, if it requires expensive changes to the plumbing and electrical systems.

■■ *Left: Experiment with different layouts to get the most from your kitchen. Here, a breakfast bar helps define the kitchen without closing it off from the sunny eating area.*
■■ *Above: Proper ventilation, provided here by an elaborately concealed vent hood, is one of the many elements needed to make a kitchen safe and efficient.*

Common Kitchen Shapes

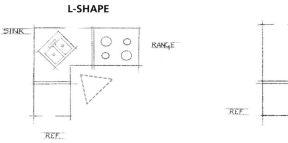

L-SHAPE

SINK

RANGE

REF.

U-SHAPE

SINK

REF.

RANGE

LARGE U-SHAPE

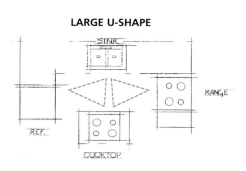

SINK

RANGE

REF.

COOKTOP

GALLEY

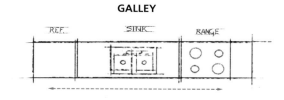

REF.   SINK   RANGE

Kitchen Design Standards

The goal of any kitchen layout is to make the cook's work easier and, where possible, to allow other people to enjoy the same space without getting in the way. Understanding the accepted kitchen design standards can help you determine whether your present layout is sufficient or if your kitchen needs a radical layout change or expansion. The most important standards are those that deal with the arrangement of the major work areas, and the sizes and placement of the countertops, appliances and cabinets.

The Work Triangle

The *work triangle* is a well-known term that describes the arrangement of the three main work areas of a kitchen—storage (refrigerator), food prep (oven and cooktop) and cleanup (sink and dishwasher). Each work area represents a "point" on the triangle, and the distance between any two points is called a "leg." Although many sources offer what may sound like rules for the work triangle, the concept is merely a planning tool for balancing the relationship of the points to one another.

Guidelines offered by the National Kitchen and Bath Association (NKBA) indicate that each leg of the triangle should be between 4 and 9 ft., the length the legs should total between 12 and 26 ft., and the arrangement of the points should discourage foot traffic through the triangle. Whenever possible, there should be a 4-ft. corridor between all stationary elements, such as a perimeter counter and an island; anything less than 3 ft. results in reduced efficiency.

Of course, not all kitchens can accommodate what might be described as an "ideal work triangle," or even a triangle at all. Some kitchens have four work stations rather than three, while others, such as galley kitchens, position all the work areas

■ *Opposite above: The most efficient kitchen layouts arrange the sink, cooktop and refrigerator in a convenient triangle.*

■ *Opposite below: Common kitchen layouts include L-shape, U-shape and galley (or corridor) plans. Larger L- and U-shaped kitchens often use an island to shorten the legs of the work triangle.*

■ *Right: In kitchens of every size, the most useful countertop space is right next to the primary work areas.*

along one wall. The important thing is not to religiously follow a set of guidelines but to create a plan that lets you work efficiently in your kitchen. For more information regarding the work triangle, contact the NKBA (page 155).

Countertops

Lack of countertop space is one of the most common complaints people have about their kitchens, but having adequate space is more than just a matter of surface area. The most useful counter spaces are those next to the main work areas and appliances. Table 1 on page 42 lists the principle kitchen appliances and the minimum recommended countertop space for each. Although standard dimensions are given for each appliance, the actual sizes of your appliances should not affect the amount of countertop space needed.

In addition to the allowances given in the table, a kitchen should have at least one uninterrupted counter surface that's at least 3 ft. long, for a food preparation area. As for overall countertop space, follow these recommendations: if your kitchen is less than 150 sq. ft., you should have at least 11 linear ft. of countertop space; if your kitchen is over 150 sq. ft., try to include at least 16 ft. 6 in. of counter space.

Use Table 2 on page 42 to calculate the amount of space you'll need for eating areas. Most eating surfaces are 30 in., 36 in. or 42 in. above the floor, and the space you need to allow for each diner varies according to the height of the surface and the type of dining.

Appliances

Any drawings you make of your kitchen should include all of the major appliances, as well as space allowances for the safe and comfortable use of each unit. If you're buying a new appliance and don't know its size, you can use the standard dimensions given in Table 1, below. Keep in mind that most appliances come in many different sizes, so you're not necessarily limited to the dimensions shown.

When placing the appliances in your kitchen layout, be sure to leave an access space of at least 30 × 48 in. in front of each appliance. Also, position each appliance so that its doors open away from traffic areas and from other appliances. The **Comments** column in Table 1 contains additional recommendations for the placement of each appliance.

Cabinets

As with countertop space, most people would like to have unlimited room for their cabinets. But kitchens have limited space, and working the cabinets into your kitchen layout can be tricky. To get an idea of how much cabinet space to include, refer to Table 3 on this page for minimums. When calculating cabinet spaces, remember to exclude any unusable corner space.

The sizes of base and wall cabinets are fairly uniform among manufacturers, and unless you have your cabinets custom-built, they'll probably follow the standards shown on page 43. (If you've already selected new cabinets, refer to the product literature for the actual dimensions.) Figure 1 on page 43 shows some general measurements to use when drawing or selecting standard base and wall cabinets.

Design Standards*

Table 1: Standard Appliance Dimensions

APPLIANCE	STANDARD DIMENSIONS (WIDTH)	MINIMUM COUNTERTOP SPACE	COMMENTS
REFRIGERATOR	30 IN. TO 36 IN.	15 IN. ON LATCH SIDE	12 CU. FT. FOR FAMILY OF FOUR; 2 CU. FT. FOR EACH ADDITIONAL PERSON
SINK	27 IN. SINGLE 36 IN. DOUBLE	24 IN. ON ONE SIDE 18 IN. ON OTHER SIDE	MINIMUM OF 3 IN. OF COUNTERTOP SPACE BETWEEN SINK AND EDGE OF BASE CABINET
RANGE	30 IN., 36 IN.	15 IN. ON ONE SIDE 9 IN. ON OTHER SIDE	IF A WINDOW IS POSITIONED ABOVE A COOKING APPLIANCE, THE BOTTOM EDGE OF THE WINDOW CASING MUST BE AT LEAST 24 IN. ABOVE THE COOKING SURFACE
COOKTOP	30 IN., 36 IN., 42 IN. 48 IN.	15 IN. ON ONE SIDE 9 IN. ON OTHER SIDE	
WALL OVEN	24 IN., 27 IN., 30 IN.	15 IN. ON EITHER SIDE	OVEN BOTTOM SHOULD BE BETWEEN 24 IN. AND 48 IN. ABOVE THE FLOOR
MICROWAVE	19 IN., 24 IN., 30 IN.	15 IN. ON EITHER SIDE	WHEN BUILT IN, PLACE LOW IN WALL CABINETS OR JUST UNDER COUNTER

Table 2: Eating Surface Standards

	HEIGHT OF EATING SURFACE		
	30 IN.	36 IN.	42 IN.
MIN. WIDTH FOR EACH SEATED DINER	30 IN.	24 IN.	24 IN.
MIN. DEPTH FOR EACH SEATED DINER	19 IN.	15 IN.	12 IN.
MINIMUM KNEE SPACE	19 IN.	15 IN.	12 IN.

Table 3: Cabinet Standards

RECOMMENDED MINIMUM FOR	SIZE OF KITCHEN	
	LESS THAN 150 SQ. FT.	MORE THAN 150 SQ. FT.
BASE CABINETS	13 LIN. FT.	16 LIN. FT.
WALL CABINETS	12 LIN. FT.	15.5 LIN. FT.
ROLL-OUT SHELVING	10 LIN. FT.	13.75 LIN. FT.

*RECOMMENDED BY THE NATIONAL KITCHEN & BATH ASSOCIATION

Building Codes

Building codes are locally enforced laws that govern building construction and renovations. They exist for your safety, and if your remodel involves anything more than refinishing the surfaces, chances are there are codes you'll need to follow. Your kitchen drawings probably won't include all of the structural and mechanical elements governed by the applicable building codes, but knowing a few of the basic guidelines can help you understand—and plan for—the various utilities that make your kitchen work. Be aware that the regulations listed here are merely general guidelines. Consult your local building department for a complete and current list of codes and regulations for your area.

Guidelines for Basic Construction

Most building codes require that a kitchen have at least one window that provides at least 10 sq. ft. of glass surface. Some localities do allow windowless kitchens, as long as the kitchen is properly vented. However, a windowless kitchen is less appealing than one that has windows or other openings to the outdoors. Kitchen designers recommend that kitchens have windows, doors or skylights that together have a total glass surface equal to at least 25% of the total floor area.

Kitchens may be required to have at least two points of entry (keep in mind that the traffic flow between them should not intrude on the work triangle). As a rule, exterior entry doors leading into a kitchen must be at least 3 ft. wide (called a three-o door) and interior passage doors between kitchens and other rooms must be at least 2½ ft. wide (called two-six doors).

■ *Left: Standard dimensions and positions for base and wall cabinets ensure a comfortable and safe work area.*

Figure 1

Shown cutaway for clarity

Maximum height 80"

12-15"

Minimum 18"

Sink

80"

36"

36" min.

3½" min.

3" min.

24"

TIP
Standard Cabinet Sizes

BASE CABINETS (WITHOUT COUNTERTOP)
height: 34½ in.
depth: 23 in.to 24 in.
width: 9 in. to 48 in., in 3 in. increments

WALL CABINETS
height: 12 in., 15 in., 18 in., 24 in., 30 in., 33 in., 42 in.
depth: 12 in.
width: 9 in. to 48 in., in 3 in. increments

OVEN CABINETS
height: 84 in., 96 in.
depth: 24 in.
width: 27 in., 30 in., 33 in.

UTILITY CABINETS
height: 84 in.
depth: 12 in., 24 in.
width: 18 in., 24 in., 36 in.

Estimating Electrical Needs

The National Electrical Code requires that all kitchens meet the following electrical guidelines:
• Wall outlets spaced no more than 6 ft. apart.
• Countertop outlets spaced no more than 2 ft. apart.
• GFCI (Ground-fault circuit interrupter) protection for all countertop receptacles.
• At least two 120-volt, 20-amp circuits; one to supply power for the refrigerator and the other for plug-in countertop appliances.
• Dedicated circuits for each major appliance. Install a 20-amp, 120-volt circuit for a built-in microwave, a 15-amp circuit for the dishwasher and food disposer. An electric range, cooktop or wall oven requires a dedicated 50-amp, 240-volt circuit.

After you estimate how much electrical service your new kitchen will need, compare it to your existing service by examining your service panel (usually located in the basement or attached garage). If the panel has a number of open slots, your electrician should be able to add additional circuits easily. If it doesn't, your new kitchen may require an upgraded service panel.

■ *Lighting and updated electrical circuits play an essential role in making a kitchen a safe and efficient place to work.*

Guidelines for Electrical Service & Lighting

Nearly any kitchen remodeling project will require some upgrading of the electrical service. While your current kitchen may be served by a single 120-volt circuit, it's not uncommon today for a large kitchen to use as many as seven individual circuits. In some cases, the additional load may mean you have to upgrade the main electrical service for the entire house.

To get an idea of how extensive your electrical improvements need to be, compare your current service with the code guidelines in **Estimating Electrical Needs** (left). Depending on the size of your project, you may want to call in an electrician to assess your current service and your planned changes.

In regard to lighting, the National Electrical Code requires only that a kitchen have some form of illumination controlled by a wall switch, but for reasons of safety, comfort and aesthetics, consider the following additions to your lighting plan:

• A general lighting circuit (120-volt, 15-amp) that operates independently from circuits that control appliances or counter receptacles

• Plentiful task lighting, including hanging lights, under-cabinet fixtures or recessed lighting, to illuminate each work area

• Decorative lighting fixtures for highlighting attractive cabinets or other features (see pages 132-135 for suggestions on designing a lighting plan).

Guidelines for Plumbing

If your new layout calls for changes with the location of the sink or if you're adding an additional sink or dishwasher, you'll need to extend your water supply and drain and vent piping.

Extending plumbing lines for a new kitchen is generally easy and inexpensive, but there are some exceptions. For example, if you're putting in an island sink, the pipes will have to be run under the floor, which is more expensive than plumbing a wall sink.

If your plumbing is more than 25 years old, your costs may go up, depending on the type and condition of your existing pipes. It's a good idea to have a plumber check out your old plumbing. Even if the new kitchen requires expensive

■ *Above: Vent hood fans are required over ranges and cooktops; they should exhaust fumes and moisture to the outdoors.*

■ *Right: Make sure your new kitchen has enough countertop outlets. Code requires that they be spaced no more than 2 ft. apart, but you may want them even closer together.*

replacement plumbing, it will be less expensive to have it done during a remodel, and it may prevent a disaster down the road. (Older plumbing may also have drain traps and vents that don't conform to current codes, and your plumber may recommend new runs here.)

Guidelines for Heating, Ventilation & Air Conditioning (HVAC) Systems

If you're planning a cosmetic make-over or a simple layout change, you can probably continue to use your existing registers or radiators. But if the new kitchen will be substantially larger, or if the ratio of glass surfaces will be greater, you may need to expand the heating/cooling system. This can be as simple as extending the ducts a few feet or as complicated as installing a new furnace to handle the additional space.

To determine your kitchen's HVAC needs, consult a professional. Although the code requirements are quite simple, HVAC contractors use a complicated formula to determine the equipment necessary to meet the code requirements.

For proper ventilation, your cooktop should be equipped with an electric vent hood to exhaust cooking fumes and moisture from the kitchen. Since the capacity of the vent is governed by code, check with a building inspector before selecting a vent hood. Many island cooktops use downdraft fans and ducts that are routed through the floor, which is a more costly and complicated job.

Create Your Drawings

Now that you're familiar with the basic principles of kitchen design, it's time to put pencil to paper. You don't need artistic skill to create useful drawings, but it helps to have some patience and a few tools and materials:

- Tape measure
- $\frac{1}{4}$ -in. graph paper
- Tracing paper
- Pens or pencils in a few different colors
- Ruler or straightedge
- Architect's ruler* (optional)

*This is marked off in various scales, so the ruler does the scaling for you (a plastic one costs a few dollars).

Use the symbols found on pages 148-149 to give your drawings a clean, uniform look. The symbols are printed to a $\frac{1}{2}$ in. = 1 ft. scale, so you can transfer them directly onto a sheet of tracing paper, which you can then use as a template.

If you find you need help with your planning or drawing, you have many options. Kitchen designers probably offer the best resource, and some provide their services on an hourly basis. Many contractors offer design assistance or can refer you to a designer they recommend. You can also ask a supplier (such as a local home center or a cabinet manufacturer) if they have a staff designer who will help with your plans if you buy your materials from them. There are even computer software programs that help with kitchen design.

You can complete as many of the following steps as you'd like. Depending on the complexity of the project and the amount of detail you're including, it may take several drafts to produce usable drawings. After you've completed your floor plans, you may want to try some front elevation drawings (Step 6). A floor plan is an *overhead* view of a room; an elevation is a *side* view of an entire wall—it's everything you see from floor to ceiling when looking in one direction. Both are two-dimensional.

Step 1. Measure everything in your present kitchen, including the overall floor and wall space, exposed flooring, cabinets, appliances, doors, windows and countertops. Also note the locations of electrical outlets, gas lines, plumbing, lighting and HVAC fixtures. Using the symbols on pages 148-149, map out your present kitchen on graph paper, scaling it $\frac{1}{2}$ in. = 1 ft.

Step 2. Lay a sheet of tracing paper over the first drawing, and begin sketching possible layouts onto the tracing paper.

Step 3. If a simple rearrangement of the layout doesn't seem to be adequate, explore the possibilities of expanding the kitchen into an adjoining room or adding to the structure. Don't be afraid to make bold changes; after all, it's only on paper at this point.

Step 4. Once you are satisfied with the layout, draw a detailed floor plan of the new kitchen on graph paper. Use dotted lines to represent base cabinets and appliances covered by countertops, and solid lines for countertops, wall cabinets and other appliances. In the margins, indicate the dimensions of each element and the distances between them.

Step 5. Use colored pens or pencils to mark the locations of all the electrical outlets and plumbing, lighting and HVAC fixtures.

Step 6. Draw a front elevation for each wall of your present kitchen or the new design. This is simple: stand squarely facing one wall, and draw an outline of everything you see (or everything you hope to see).

■ *If you've selected some new products, refer to the manufacturers' literature for exact dimensions to use in your drawings.*

TIP

Creating Plan Drawings

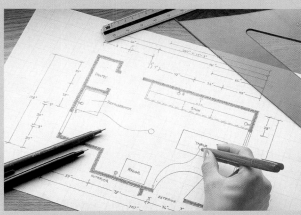

Step 1. Carefully measure your present kitchen, then draw a scaled plan that shows every feature of the room.

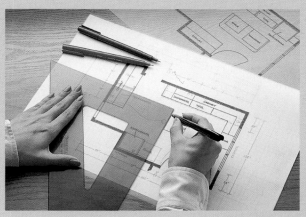

Step 2. Lay tracing paper over the original floor plan and experiment with layouts for your new kitchen.

Step 3. Consider major layout changes, perhaps including a room addition.

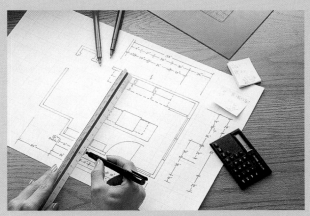

Step 4. Create a new floor plan of your design. Use solid and dotted lines to distinguish elements.

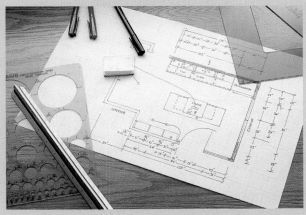

Step 5. Complete the floor plan by marking the locations of all electrical, plumbing and HVAC fixtures.

Step 6. Create front elevation drawings for each wall in your present or planned kitchen.

FINDING THE FINANCING

ny successful kitchen remodel starts with dreams and becomes reality. Which means that at some point, after you've spent time wishing and dreaming, you'll have to figure out where reality lies for you. Dream kitchens can be expensive—very expensive, in some cases. But before you panic, take a deep breath and read this chapter. You'll discover many practical ways to control costs and reduce the financial sting of remodeling.

Although you probably have an idea of how much you'd like to spend on your dream kitchen, you're likely to find that the figure is too small to cover everything you want. To avoid disappointment later, you might as well know up front: when budgeting for a kitchen remodel, you need to be prepared to pay a bit more than you've planned and be willing to settle for a bit less than you've dreamed. Compromise is inevitable in the remodeling process, but with perseverance and a bit of luck, you can spend reasonably and still end up with a beautiful new kitchen that you'll love to use.

■ *Left: If you start with a realistic budget and look for creative ways to reduce costs, you should be able to save enough money to afford the design options you really want.*
■ *Above: Don't assume you can't afford to remodel your kitchen until you've checked out every financing option—you may be surprised at just how many options exist.*

Budgeting

Establishing a budget is an important step in the remodeling process, and it involves more than determining how much money you have, or want, to spend. Additional factors, including the current value of your home and how long you plan to stay there, will have bearing on your budgeting decisions and will help you set a sensible budget goal.

Setting a Budget Goal

How much should you spend on your kitchen project? Real estate professionals offer the following rough guidelines, based on the market value of your home before the remodel and the complexity of your project (see **The Five Levels of Kitchen Remodeling**, pages 36-37):

• For a full kitchen remodeling job with a general contractor (Levels 2-4), plan to spend 10% to 20% of your home's value ($15,000 to $30,000 for a $150,000 home).

• For a Level 5 project, plan to spend up to 35% of your home's value ($52,500 for a $150,000 home).

• For a Level 1 cosmetic makeover, plan to spend at least 2% of your home's value ($3,000 for a $150,000 home).

Do these sound like huge sums of money? There are good reasons to invest in a new kitchen. A remodeled kitchen is one of the few home improvements that translates directly into a higher market value for your home—industry figures indicate that you can expect to recoup 85% to 110% of the money invested in a Level 1 project, and between 60% and 85% for a Level 2, 3 or 4 project. Even if you plan to sell in the near future, you'll enjoy the improvements until that time, and the kitchen's new look may help make the sale when the

■ *In addition to increasing the livability of one of the most important rooms in your house, a kitchen remodel can immediately increase your home's market value.*

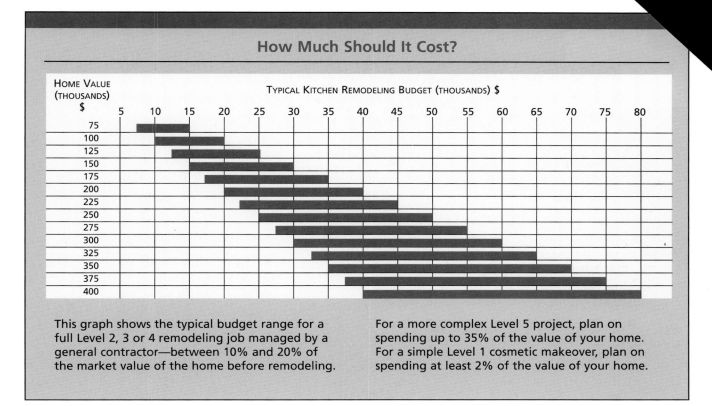

How Much Should It Cost?

HOME VALUE (THOUSANDS) $	TYPICAL KITCHEN REMODELING BUDGET (THOUSANDS) $

This graph shows the typical budget range for a full Level 2, 3 or 4 remodeling job managed by a general contractor—between 10% and 20% of the market value of the home before remodeling.

For a more complex Level 5 project, plan on spending up to 35% of the value of your home. For a simple Level 1 cosmetic makeover, plan on spending at least 2% of the value of your home.

time comes. However, it's probably wise to scale back on the project if you plan to sell immediately (see page 35).

If you'll be keeping your home for many years, the investment risk of the project lies in your enjoyment of the new kitchen. But with thoughtful planning and careful selection of appliances and materials, you're sure to get a great return on your investment over the years.

While it may be best to pay for a remodel with disposable income—that is, accumulated savings—there are several legitimate ways to pay for an improvement project, and even more ways to reduce and manage the cost of a new kitchen.

Estimating Costs

Begin your budgeting process by estimating the cost of your ideal kitchen, as you've envisioned it so far.

Create a Rough Estimate

Use **Worksheet 3** on page 150 to record the estimated cost of each element you'd like to have in your new kitchen. For more information on your options for appliances, countertops, cabinets and other materials, refer to Part II of this book.

Next, use the chart, **Estimating Kitchen Remodeling Costs** (page 52), to calculate rough cost estimates. Note

that the cost figures for products and services reflect a wide range; to develop more precise estimates, check the prices in appliance stores and building centers, and ask contractors about their rates. Also add any additional labor charges you expect, such as interior design, cleanup help and trash hauling.

Finally, total all your costs, then add a 10% to 20% contingency fund to the total. The contingency fund is essential: few remodeling projects come in exactly on budget, and it's difficult to list every expense at this stage, so keep your estimates on the high side to avoid any unpleasant surprises.

Use Your Rough Estimate

Don't panic when you see the total; your first rough estimate is simply a starting point. In addition, it can help you answer some crucial questions:

• Is your rough estimate within the recommended ratio of your home's market value? If it exceeds the range shown above, look for ways to reduce your budget.

• Should you do the work yourself, or hire a contractor? Check the entries in the last column of **Estimating Kitchen Remodeling Costs** (page 52)—the labor-to-materials ratio. The elements with the highest labor cost offer the greatest potential savings if you do the work

Estimating Kitchen Remodeling Costs

	COST RANGE (INSTALLED)	LABOR/MATERIALS RATIO
General contractor	10% to 20% of total project cost	
Kitchen designer	$1,000 to $8,000	
Architect	$2,000 to $10,000	
Construction of addition	$70 to $120/sq. ft.	50/50
Doors, windows		
exterior door	$300 to $1,200	50/50
interior door	$100 to $350	50/50
patio door	$1,000 to $2,500	35/65
window, standard	$400 to $1,000	40/60
window, bay	$2,000 to $5,000	50/50
skylight	$500 to $2,500	50/50
Cabinets & trim, stock	$100 to $350/lin. ft.	20/80
Cabinets, custom-built	$400 to $600/lin. ft.	30/70
Appliances & fixtures		
sink (faucet, plumbing)	$300 to $1,000	30/70
range	$400 to $2,000	10/90
cooktop	$200 to $1,200	10/90
wall oven	$700 to $3,000	10/90
refrigerator	$600 to $3,000	10/90
microwave	$200 to $400	10/90
garbage disposer	$150 to $300	50/50
dishwasher	$400 to $950	25/75
trash compactor	$200 to $400	25/75
vent hood & ducts	$350 to $1,000	30/70
Countertops		
laminate	$20 to $50/lin. ft.	25/75
ceramic tile	$5 to $30/sq. ft.	50/50
solid-surface	$100 to $150/lin. ft.	15/85
stainless steel	$70 to $140/lin. ft.	20/80
Flooring		
vinyl	$3 to $15/sq. ft.	25/75
hardwood	$5 to $15/sq. ft.	40/60
ceramic tile	$5 to $30/sq. ft.	50/50
laminate	$8 to $20/sq. ft.	40/60
Electrical		
electrical outlets	$35 to $80	75/25
appliance circuit	$150 to $200	75/25
electric baseboard heat	$40 to $50/lin. ft.	10/90
lighting fixture	$30 to $300	10/90
Wall, ceiling surfaces		
drywall	$.75 to $3/sq. ft.	65/35
plaster	$30 to $40/sq. yd.	80/20
paneling	$3 to $20/sq. ft.	40/60
ceramic tile	$5 to $20/sq. ft.	50/50
Walls, finish		
paint	$.06 to $.15/sq. ft.	80/20
wallpaper	$1 to $5/sq. ft.	50/50

Estimates based on 1997 market data.

yourself. In most cases, however, there are reasons why labor costs are high, so you should consider doing work yourself only if you're experienced and confident that you can successfully complete the job.

• Are you getting accurate bids? If a contractor submits a bid that's much higher or lower than the ranges shown, ask why (see **Hiring Professionals,** page 59).

Reducing Costs

At this point you should have a rough idea of how much your dream kitchen will cost. Are you already over your budget? If so, don't worry; the first estimate often exceeds the budget. That's why you're figuring costs before you get started—it allows you to make carefully planned cutbacks now, which may save you from having to make drastic ones later. There are several ways to begin lowering your remodeling costs.

Change the Scope of the Project

Any remodeling project that involves building a room addition or moving interior walls will be expensive. If your initial vision included this kind of expansion, take another look to see if it's really necessary. If you can get by with a room rearrangement or a cosmetic makeover, your costs will go down considerably.

Adjust Your Priorities

Your new kitchen needs to meet your practical needs and expectations, of course—but a remodeling project can sometimes go far beyond that, to become an exercise in vanity. This is the time to reevaluate your choices and decide which elements are truly important and which you can do without.

To do this, rank the items on your wish list in order of importance and evaluate where you want to make the biggest investment. Are granite countertops really essential, or would you rather spend that money on a laminate floor? Can you live without a bay window if it means you can afford better cabinets with convenient accessories?

Comparison-Shop for Materials

If your heart is set on premium-quality materials, do some homework to make sure you're getting the best price you can. If the best price is still too high, bear in

mind that good-quality materials can be just as serviceable as top-of-the-line luxury products.

If possible, buy your appliances during the end-of-year close-out sales, which are usually held in January and February. However, don't get so wrapped up in saving money that you forget to make sure that the appliances match one another.

Although contractors and subcontractors will purchase appliances and materials for you, this service isn't free; they typically take a markup on every item they buy. It's often cheaper to research and purchase the materials yourself.

Finally, you can save the costs of delivering many remodeling materials if you have access to a truck and are able to transport them yourself.

Comparison-Shop for Contractors

While cost shouldn't be your first consideration when looking for a contractor, it's an important one for most people. But if you want to reduce your total labor expense, it's better to cut back on service rather than on the contractor's experience and abilities. If you are somewhat flexible with time and can live with less than a "full-service" treatment, a small, or "independent," contractor might be better (and cheaper) for you than a large contracting organization.

■ *January and February are good times to shop for appliances and some fixtures, because that's when many manufacturers close out last year's models.*

Regardless of the contractor's reputation or how much he or she charges, always check references. Whenever possible, talk to several recent customers and visit some completed job sites. As the saying goes, "The best predictor of future success is past performance."

Do Some Work Yourself

Since labor is often the most expensive element of a remodeling project, you may be able to save money by doing parts of the job yourself. However, make sure you're up to the task (see **Hiring Professionals,** page 59). Don't plan to build your own cabinetry if you don't have a lot of experience with a table saw, and don't plan to install your plumbing if sweating a copper pipe fitting isn't second nature. Tackle only those tasks that you're confident you can complete successfully.

Many homeowners do only the preliminary demolition and the final painting and trim work themselves, leaving all the other tasks to professionals. However, even this do-it-yourself labor requires extra time in your remodel-ing schedule. A job that can be done in a single afternoon by a professional carpenter will probably take you at least two or three days, even if you have the right skills. Also, bear in mind that contractors don't always welcome homeowner participation, often with good reason. To avoid any problems with your contractors, let them know what jobs you'd like to do yourself.

Financing

Once you've reduced the cost estimate to a comfortable amount, it's time to consider where the money will come from. The following are seven of the most common methods of financing a major remodeling project. Some methods of financing involve considerable paperwork that can take several weeks to process, so the sooner you start, the better. Use **Worksheet 4** (page 151) to record the information that lenders will ask for when you apply for a loan.

Out-of-Pocket Funds

The ideal way to pay for a remodeling project is to use accumulated savings. The advantage of this method is that you don't have to pay any loan interest, which can mean a savings of thousands of dollars. For example, when you borrow $25,000 at 10% interest and pay it off over 10 years, you actually end up paying over $39,000—the cost of the loan plus over $14,000 in interest.

Although paying out-of-pocket is cheaper in the long run, it has one significant drawback: If the actual costs far exceed your estimates, you

■ *Replacing kitchen walls with an island is one way to create a more expansive feeling without the extra costs involved in an addition or expansion project.*

could end up in a pay-as-you-go situation, and the project would take a lot longer to complete. A sizable kitchen remodel could easily take many months to complete if you're paying for it by squeezing a little bit from each paycheck.

You can avoid this problem by delaying the start of the project until you've saved more than enough money to pay for it. Plan a starting date a year or two in the future, make up a schedule for saving the money, and stick to it. As you watch your funds grow, you can entertain yourself by shopping for bargains on discontinued appliances and other materials. Just make sure you have enough space to store your purchases until the work begins.

Revolving Credit

If you're thinking of using credit cards to pay the bills for your new kitchen, think again. Unless it's absolutely unavoidable, resist all temptations to pull out the plastic when remodeling your kitchen. The interest rates on credit cards, which typically range from 12% to 25%, are far higher than other financing options. This will add thousands of dollars to the cost of your project, and none of the interest is tax deductible.

If you need to charge appliances or other materials to your credit cards, make sure you pay down these debts as quickly as possible. As any financial adviser will tell you, it's only too easy to end up burdened for years with thousands of dollars in credit card debt.

Government-Backed Loans

There are a number of programs that you may be able to turn to for help financing your remodeling project. Two popular federal programs are the Title 1 Property Improvement Loan program and the 203K plan. Both loan plans are administered through lenders approved by the FHA (Federal Housing Administration). To find qualified lenders, contact your local HUD (Housing & Urban Development) field office. The interest rates and payback schedules for these government-backed loans are about the same as conventional mortgages.

The maximum amount a homeowner can borrow under Title 1 changes each year—for current information, contact your lender. Loans less than $5,000 require only a good credit record, but larger loans must be secured with collateral, usually a lien on your home. Interest rates for these loans are determined by your lender and are based on current market rates.

The 203K plan allows you to refinance your home and

TIP

Payback Common Sense

To save money, pay back loans as quickly as you can, especially if the interest isn't tax deductible. When you take out any loan, the total cost (principal plus interest) of the loan depends primarily on how long you take to pay it back. Before you pay off a loan, however, make sure it doesn't carry a penalty for early repayment. In general, avoid taking out any loan that has an early-repayment penalty.

---

secure a remodeling loan with a single mortgage package. To qualify, you must live in a stable neighborhood, your plans must include changes that will increase the market value of your home (such as an addition), and the cost of the project must be at least $5,000.

Securing a government-backed loan can be a lengthy process. You'll need to to submit detailed bids for the project from FHA-approved contractors. The lender will usually also require an independent appraisal of your home and your neighborhood.

Mortgage Refinancing

Converting an old mortgage to a new loan is a common way to finance a new kitchen. This option is especially advisable if current interest rates are 1% or more below the rate of your old mortgage, and you have a sizable amount of equity in your home. Refinancing is also a good choice if you're doing a costly project that will add considerably to the market value of your home.

One potential benefit of refinancing your current mortgage is that you may be able to take a tax deduction on the interest you pay on the loan. Ask a mortgage company or bank about the current tax laws regarding mortgage loans; then consult your tax advisor.

Refinancing can be a time-consuming process involving lots of paperwork. And since the collateral for a refinanced mortgage is your home itself, lenders will generally ask for an independent appraisal of your property to ensure its value is sufficient to secure the loan.

Any local mortgage company or full-service bank can help you arrange a refinanced mortgage. But it's best to shop around, as mortgage interest rates vary from lender to lender. The typical payback schedules are 15, 20, 25 and 30 years. Another good source for loan information is the Internet (see page 155 for some helpful web sites).

■ *You may have the skills to install your own kitchen floor and save the cost of a professional installation.*

Home Equity Loans

If you prefer not to refinance your existing mortgage, you can opt to borrow money against your home equity—the difference between your home's market value and the amount you owe on your mortgage. For example, if your home is worth $150,000 and your remaining mortgage balance is $100,000, you have $50,000 in home equity; you can use much of this money to serve as collateral for a loan. Find out the outstanding balance on your mortgage by calling your lender.

There are two types of home equity loans. The first is a simple second mortgage, in which you borrow a lump sum at a fixed interest rate and pay it back in regular installments over a period of 15 years or more. The second is an equity line of credit.

Equity credit lines operate like revolving credit card accounts, in which you borrow money when you need it and pay interest on the outstanding balance. The interest rates on these loans vary with the market rates, so your payments may change from month to month. Like credit cards, equity credit accounts can be dangerous if you aren't a disciplined borrower.

■ *Budgeting is a tradeoff. What you don't spend on layout changes, you may want put toward better cabinets or fixtures.*

Life Insurance Policies

Many whole-life or other types of permanent life insurance policies allow you to borrow against the cash value of the policy. In most cases, getting the money is a simple matter of requesting and filling out a loan application, and the entire process is generally quite speedy. Your original insurance contract should include a fixed interest rate you pay on this type of loan. Depending on the interest rates current when you take out the loan, your fixed rate may be considerably lower. However, the interest paid on insurance loans is not tax deductible.

It's also possible to cancel and cash out your life insurance policies, in which case the money is yours to spend as you like. Before you cash out, however, check with your insurance agent. There may be penalties for early withdrawal, as well as taxes on any investment income generated within the policy. Also be aware that if you terminate your policy now, then get hurt or sick, you may have difficulty getting life insurance in the future.

Retirement Funds

Many 401K and other company-sponsored retirement programs allow you to borrow against the money in your account. The interest rates for these loans are determined by current interest rates, and if the money is used for home improvement, the payback schedule may be as long as 30 years.

Contact your financial advisor or your company human resources department for information on borrowing from retirement funds. These loans are usually repaid by automatic payroll deductions. However, bear in mind that if you leave your job for any reason and fail to pay back the loan, the outstanding balance will immediately be viewed as taxable income by the IRS.

Home Improvement Loans

This is the standard, everyday bank loan—the same type of loan you would use to buy a car. Any full-service bank or credit union can process a home improvement loan. The advantage of a home improvement loan is that it can be processed very quickly, no appraisal is needed and little paperwork is involved, other than a quick computerized credit check. The drawback is that the interest rates are generally 2% to 5% higher than the current rates for home equity loans.

Since home improvement loans are generally secured by your home, the interest may be tax deductible. Ask your lender about the tax laws specific to your loan. You can also use other property, such as savings bonds, as collateral for the loan, but in this case the interest may not be tax deductible. The payback time on a home improvement loan is generally 10 years or less.

■ *The price of light fixtures can vary widely; you may be able to squeeze your budget without sacrificing the look you want.*

Personal Loans

Borrowing money from friends or relatives is another possibility, but it's one that requires careful consideration. Too often, personal loans are made on the basis of a handshake and a verbal promise, and this kind of arrangement can easily lead to hard feelings and even legal problems.

When structured correctly, however, a personal loan can benefit both you and the lender: A personal loan can be financed at an interest rate that's lower than you could borrow from a bank, but higher than your lender could earn in a savings account or bond fund. And if you secure the loan against your home with a deed of trust contract, you may be allowed to take a tax deduction on some of the interest you pay.

If you borrow money from a friend or relative, it's essential to put your agreement in writing as a legal document, with all the details spelled out. How long will you take to pay back the money? Will you pay it back in installments, or in one lump sum? How much interest will you pay on the loan? Are you securing the loan with a deed of trust against your home? If you approach a personal loan in the same way as a formal bank loan, you're more likely to stay in the good graces of your kindly lender.

■ *When adding an eating area, remember to consider the cost of new furniture, window treatments and room decor.*

HIRING PROFESSIONALS

When it comes to hiring professionals for help with home improvements, few homeowners have done it enough to become experts. Many people dread this part of the process; it puts them on edge because they're afraid they'll be taken advantage of. Although general awareness and careful scrutiny are important, finding the best professionals for your project is primarily a matter of asking the right questions. Before any work starts, it's essential that both parties know exactly what is to be done and how much money is involved.

Depending on the size of your kitchen remodel, you may be hiring professionals from several different fields, such as designers, carpenters, plumbers and flooring installers. Some hiring decisions will simply be based on your budget or on your skills as a do-it-yourselfer.

Start by identifying the kind of help you need—then ask around for referrals of reputable contractors. If you're managing the job yourself, you'll need to interview with many different subcontractors to find the best person for each job. On the other hand, if you hire a general contractor the rest of the hiring will be done for you, so finding the right person for that job is critical.

This chapter walks you through the entire hiring process, from finding prospective contractors and conducting the first interviews to making sure that the contracts you sign leave nothing to chance.

■ *Opposite: In addition to electricians, carpenters and plumbers, remodeling this kitchen required the services of subcontractors who specialize in installing solid surface countertops and ceramic tile flooring.* ■ *Above: Plumbing a new kitchen island is a complicated job that requires skilled professionals.*

Remodeling Professionals

Most of the major remodeling trades fall into three categories: design, management, and building/installation. It's best to familiarize yourself with each trade, and consider how each one might contribute to your project.

Design Professionals

Designers specialize in turning your rough ideas into working plans or blueprints for actual construction. They work under different professional labels and generally command substantial fees for their time.

Kitchen designers specialize in planning kitchen spaces. As a group, they offer a wide range of services, from helping you choose colors to acting as general contractors. There are many kitchen design firms out there as well as individuals, and it's important to find the right one for your project. Start by looking for designers who are certified by the National Kitchen and Bath Association (look for the initials "CKD," meaning "Certified Kitchen Designer"). You can contact the NKBA to get a list of certified designers in your area (see page 155). Kitchen designers charge their fees in a variety of ways. Some charge a flat fee or charge by the

■ *An architect is helpful when you're planning a kitchen expansion involving significant structural changes.*

hour (about $40-$100 per hour). Depending on what kind of help they give you, designers may charge a percentage of the project materials or the total project cost. Using a designer often results in a close working relationship, so be sure to interview several candidates before hiring one.

Interior designers are designers at a more general level: they work with all areas of the home. They can help you choose materials and appliances to achieve a specific mood or style. Designers generally charge between $40 and $80 per hour, plus a percentage of the cost of interior finishes and furnishings. However, some very talented designers work for building contractors, custom-cabinet firms and home centers. Before hiring an independent designer, find out if your general contractor, building contractor or cabinetmaker can provide this service at a lower cost.

Architects are licensed professionals who design and prepare detailed construction plans for homes and buildings. An architect may be helpful if you're planning radical changes, such as removing or adding exterior walls, building an addition, or vaulting a ceiling. Architects charge substantially for their expertise, and only the most complex projects warrant this kind of help. They generally charge either a percentage of the budget (8% to 15%) or an hourly rate ($80 to $200 per hour).

Building designers have similar skills to architects, but usually don't have as much engineering background. Although they charge less ($60 to $100 per hour), most have extensive experience in construction and design. Many building design companies offer design, project management and a construction specialty. A building designer is a good choice if your plans call for extensive redesign work.

Design/Build Firms are companies that offer a complete remodeling package in one service. They have their own designers and contractors who work together to complete the project from the first stages of drawing the plans to the final finish construction and decorating. In most cases, you'll pay one fee for this "turnkey" service.

Management Professionals

General contractors are professional remodeling managers who hire, schedule, coordinate and supervise the activities of all the other professionals working on a remodeling project. General contractors can make a large, complicated job much easier for you, since they'll hire and schedule the subcontractors and serve as the liaison between you and the other workers. However, this convenience comes at a price—either a flat fee or a percentage of the budget. A reputable general contractor typically charges 10% to 20% of the total construction cost. Also, many general contractors will only take on projects with a total cost over $8,000 to $10,000; smaller projects don't offer them enough profit. If your kitchen project falls below this range, perhaps you can hire a kitchen design firm to manage the project or you can manage it yourself.

Building & Installation Professionals

These tradespeople provide the actual hands-on labor needed to complete your kitchen remodel. If you manage the project yourself, you'll need to hire and supervise them directly.

Carpenters handle many different building tasks, such as tearing down walls, adding beams and partitions, and framing new walls,

windows and doors. Many carpenters will do both the rough carpentry and the finish work, including installing cabinets, trim and some countertops and flooring.

Plumbers plan and route the water supply and the drain, waste and vent pipes from the existing lines to the new fixtures. In some areas, plumbers also make gas connections for a range, oven or cooktop, and they may hook up appliances, like dishwashers, food disposers and refrigerator icemakers. However, if you buy a large appliance, such as a dishwasher or refrigerator, the installation may be included in the delivery cost. Some plumbers are also boiler contractors (see below).

HVAC (Heating, Ventilation and Air Conditioning) *contractors* route duct work for forced-air heating and air-conditioning systems and cooktop hoods, and they add new heating and air-conditioning registers.

Boiler contractors are needed if you have an older home with a steam heating system or a hydronically (hot water) heated home. A boiler contractor will install new radiators and pipe runs if your project includes a heated room addition.

Electricians install wiring, circuits, outlets and lighting fixtures. They add electric baseboard heaters and hard-wired large appliances, such as electric ranges. They can also upgrade your old wiring and electrical circuits.

Drywall installers hang, tape and finish drywall so it's

■ *A kitchen designer can help clarify your ideas and add a professional touch to the look of your remodeled kitchen.*

Talk to Building inspectors

Although building inspectors aren't paid consultants, they can be an excellent design and planning resource. They are your community's field representatives, and their job is to inspect the work done on your project to ensure that it meets building code requirements.

As experts in their respective fields, the building inspector, electrical inspector and plumbing inspector can give you sound advice on designing your kitchen. Not all inspectors have the time or the willingness to answer a lot of design questions, so make your questions short and specific, and be sure to describe your situation clearly. Also ask if the inspections office provides a pamphlet that summarizes the local code requirements for kitchens.

smooth and ready for paint or wallpaper. Some homeowners choose to install the drywall themselves, then hire a professional to tape and finish it. Some drywall installers also texture walls and ceilings or do painting and wallpapering.

Painters and *wallpaper hangers* complete new wall surfaces. Some also stain and finish wood surfaces.

Flooring installers remove existing flooring and subfloors, prepare underlayment, and install new flooring. Many installers specialize in only one type of flooring.

Tile installers (or tile *setters*) install tile of all types. Depending on the application, they may create a mortar base or install and prepare a backer board foundation for the tile, or they may lay the tile over existing drywall or other surface.

Custom cabinetmakers design and build tailor-made kitchen cabinets and install them.

General laborers do unskilled manual labor, such as demolition, cleanup, delivering and moving building supplies. If you have teenage children, you may wish to enlist their help, or you can hire college students to help out. General laborers typically earn $8 to $16 per hour.

Do It Yourself?

You may want to hire professionals for every aspect of your remodeling project—or you may be thinking that you can save huge amounts of money by doing everything yourself. Both approaches can work, but not very often. If you never put on work gloves, you may always wonder how much money you might have saved. And if you attempt to shoulder the entire burden, you may be so shaken by the experience that you never attempt another remodeling project.

The homeowners who end up happiest tend to be those who were willing to pitch in, but were wise enough to call in help when needed. Although there's no hard and fast rule about which jobs you should tackle yourself, here are some points to consider:

Be Your Own Designer

It's often best to do the preliminary designing and planning work yourself—in fact, if you've followed the instructions in the earlier chapters of this book, you've done much of it already. Although a good designer may be able to do amazing things with your kitchen space, it will probably cost you at least $1,000 to have one design your kitchen.

Another option is to find a designer who will work with you on an hourly basis and help fine tune a design you have created. You can also consult a designer at a home center—often for free. If you've hired a general contractor or any subcontractors, remember that they, too, may be very knowledgeable and helpful when it comes to planning and layout issues.

Be Your Own General Contractor

Some homeowners may want to take on the role of general contractor and manage their own kitchen remodeling project, which can reduce the costs by $3,000 or more. As your own general contractor, you'll hire and schedule all the subcontractors needed for the project. Although you'll have the burden of hiring all the workers, you'll also have the opportunity to hand-pick the people who'll work on your kitchen.

Managing the project yourself makes sense if your schedule is flexible and you don't need to have the work done by a specific deadline. However, acting as your own general contractor can be quite an undertaking, especially if the project is large or complicated. Before you decide to take on the role of general contractor, make sure you have the following knowledge, skills and abilities:

• *Organization.* A major remodeling project is a complicated affair that requires systematic organization of many details.

• *Remodeling knowledge.* To supervise the job and approve the work of subcontractors and laborers, you'll need a good understanding of the work they're doing.

• *Bookkeeping and math skills.* Keeping tabs on the budget and organizing receipts and expenditures is an essential aspect of managing the job.

• *A strong personality.* At some point, you'll need to be firm with subcontractors or suppliers. You don't need to be hostile, but you can't be passive, either.

• *Integrity.* You can't demand excellence from your subcontractors unless you treat them honestly, make decisions they rely on quickly and effectively and pay them on time. Some subcontractors refuse to work with homeowner general contractors—you may need to convince them that you're prepared to handle the job professionally.

Do Some of the Work Yourself

Another way to save a few bucks is to do some of the physical labor yourself. Even if you've hired a general contractor to manage the project, you may be able to arrange to do some of the simpler jobs. Here are some labor-intensive tasks you may want to consider doing:

Demolition work involves removing old cabinetry, countertops, floor surfaces and

■ *The general contractor's job is to keep all subcontractors and tradespeople on schedule and on budget. If you don't have a general contractor, this will be your responsibility.*

non load-bearing interior walls. This work can be time-consuming, but it's not very difficult. However, it's important that you know what you're doing. Mistakes made during demolition can delay the job and compromise the finished product. If you're working with subcontractors, make sure they know exactly what work you'll be doing. It is also helpful to understand the construction steps that will follow the demolition work, which can save you from the common pitfall of demolishing too much.

Safety is another important concern in demolition work. Always wear sturdy work boots, gloves, eye protection and a dust mask or respirator. And take special care to find out what's behind any wall or other surface, such as electrical wiring and plumbing pipes, before cutting into it. There are many do-it-yourself books on construction and remodeling that can show you how to do this safely. Or, ask a professional.

Adding insulation and vapor barriers to new walls is a relatively easy job. Plan to do this after the wiring and plumbing are completed, but before the drywall installers arrive. Always follow the manufacturers' instructions.

Painting interior walls is well within the ability of most homeowners. You can also save a little bit by purchasing the painting supplies yourself.

■ *Most homeowners can tackle jobs such as demolition, installing insulation, painting and cleanup.*

Finishing touches, such as adjusting cabinet doors and hardware and filling nail holes on woodwork are normally done by a carpenter, but you can do this work yourself. This also gives you a chance to inspect the work and bring any problems to the attention of the contractor before you make your final payment.

Cleanup is an ongoing job that can save you a surprising amount of money. When negotiating bids with contractors, offer to take care of the cleanup in exchange for a reduced fee. When the project is under way, plan to do some cleanup work almost every day. If you expect large amounts of refuse, have a dumpster on site. Otherwise, check with your local waste-removal provider for any restrictions on the disposal of construction waste.

Use Your Specialized Skills

If you have considerable experience performing some of the more technical remodeling jobs, such as carpentry, plumbing and wiring, you may choose to do these tasks yourself. However, keep the following points in mind:

First, make sure you're qualified to do the work properly. Building inspectors will carefully scrutinize any work you do yourself, so you'll need to demonstrate that you know exactly what you're doing. In addition, substandard work on any step of the project can undermine the work of your subcontractors. For example, you can't

hold your drywall contractor accountable for bad results if you're the one responsible for framing crooked walls.

Finally, schedule extra time for any work you're doing yourself. Although a licensed electrician can easily wire a kitchen in an afternoon, an experienced do-it-yourselfer may need two or three days to complete the same job. Be realistic about your abilities, limitations and available time.

Think Twice About These Jobs

There are some jobs—such as finishing woodwork, hanging drywall or installing vinyl sheet flooring—that look like do-it-yourself projects until you realize that the fees involved are extremely reasonable compared to the time, effort and frustration involved in doing it yourself.

For example, a $500 fee for drywall installation and finishing sounds like a great bargain to anyone who's ever spent eight miserable days trying to get it right. The fees of vinyl flooring installers are similarly reasonable, especially since they have the tools and skills to do the job very quickly. Finishing woodwork is also more time-consuming and difficult than most people realize—and it can be hazardous as well, since the vapors may be toxic and flammable. If possible, leave this work to a professional.

Hanging wallpaper and installing ceramic tile are two more tasks that can be extremely time-consuming and frustrating for a nonprofessional. If your project includes these jobs, you may find that hiring professional help is well worth the expense.

Hiring Contractors

Once you've identified what kind of help you need, the next step is to find qualified professionals, interview them, check their backgrounds and references and formalize your partnership with a legal contract.

Begin by focusing on the trades that constitute the most important and complex aspects of your remodeling project. A skilled custom cabinetmaker, for example, is much harder to find than a journeyman plumber. In these specialty trades, the very best subcontractors are in high demand, especially if they have unique abilities; you'll want to hire them and lock them into your schedule as soon as possible. Once your primary subcontractors are in place, it's generally not as difficult to find plumbers, electricians and laborers to fit your schedule.

Finding Good Contractors

Word-of-mouth is usually the best way to find good subcontractors. Ask neighbors, friends, coworkers and relatives who have finished a remodeling project to recommend good professionals and warn you about those to avoid. Many of the finest tradespeople don't advertise at all; they rely exclusively on word-of-mouth.

Another option is to contact a full-service kitchen design center or a design/build firm; both can provide nearly any contractor you might need, from a general contractor to painting and wallpapering workers. However, this service is generally reserved for paying clients.

Many building supply centers are also entering the remodeling business as a way to sell materials; for a price, they will supply you with a list of local contractors. Also, builders' associations and local trade guilds often publish lists of qualified contractors.

Finally, you can consult the Yellow Pages. Look under each trade—such as Contractors (General), Building Contractors, Electrical Contractors or Kitchen Remodeling. This can be risky, however, so be sure to scrutinize any contractor you find in the Yellow Pages—especially those not endorsed by word-of-mouth or a reputable organization.

In general, look for a contractor who's based relatively close to your home. A local contractor with an established business relies heavily on his or her reputation in the community and is therefore likely to take your job seriously. Also look for a contractor who has a lot of experience with projects similar to yours in size and complexity. Before you make any calls, you can weed out contractors who aren't insured, as well as those who aren't licensed—if that's required in your area. You can ask to see proof that the contractor meets these requirements at your first interview (see page 66).

■ *If you have the skills to complete some of the specialized tasks yourself, be sure your work is accurate and timely.*

Once you find a contractor you trust to do one part of the project, you should ask him to recommend other professionals. For example, a good carpenter will probably know skilled electricians, cabinetmakers, plumbers and flooring contractors.

Conducting the Initial Interview

In your initial phone calls to prospective contractors, your goal is to create a short list of those suitable for further consideration and to exclude those who don't fit your needs. For example, you may quickly disqualify some because they aren't available when you need them. You may also intuitively sense whether a contractor is someone with whom you can work comfortably. Trust your instincts on this; a contractor who's surly in your first conversation is unlikely to grow more cooperative as the project develops.

If the initial phone call is promising, invite the contractor to your home to discuss the required work. To ensure a productive meeting, have ready as much information as possible. Floor plan drawings (if you have any) can help a contractor give you an accurate estimate. In addition, provide any other drawings and lists of materials, cabinets, appliances and fixtures involved. Given enough detailed information, the contractor may be able to offer you a firm price quote at the first interview. If you're looking for ways to reduce costs, this is also the time to offer to do some of the work in

■ *The Yellow Pages can help you find contractors in your area, but be sure to check the references and credit of any contractor who comes without a personal recommendation.*

exchange for a lower price.

Although selecting the best contractors can be a time-consuming process, resist the urge to hurry it along. Depending on the scope of your project, you may be hiring as many as five or six subcontractors. For each one, you should interview at least three candidates. By the end of each interview, you should have the following information from each one:

• *Number of years in business.* Whenever possible, use a contractor who has been in business in your community for at least five years.

• *Operating license number.* Many states require skilled tradespeople to be officially licensed. If this is the case in your area, avoid contractors who aren't licensed.

• *Insurance information.* Make sure that each contractor is insured against accidental injury to his or her workers. You'll also need to see proof of liability insurance, which covers any damage to your property. Request to see certificates from the insurance companies as proof of current coverage.

• *Bonding information.* A performance bond is a type of insurance that protects a contractor against legal action from a client who's unhappy with his or her work. While bonding is uncommon in residential construction, and is therefore not an important criterion, it does indicate that the contractor has earned the confidence of his or her insurance company.

• *Suppliers.* Find out where the contractor buys materials. This can tell you something about the quality of the

materials and enables you to call the suppliers to check the contractor's credit history.

• *References.* Ask for the names of the contractor's last 10 to 20 clients, including at least one job that's still under way, if possible. It won't be necessary to contact this many clients, but having more references allows you to conduct a random check. Avoid any contractor who's unable or unwilling to provide you with these references.

• *Price quote.* Although the difference may seem subtle, in the remodeling business an estimate is quite different from a quote or a bid. An estimate is simply the contractor's best guess of how much the job will cost, while a quote is a firm price submitted after careful consideration. Never hire a contractor on the basis of an informal estimate.

When hiring subcontractors, they may offer to work based on "time and materials." The time (labor) will be accounted for and charged out at an agreed upon rate; materials will be billed according to what's used. Be sure to ask if the materials are being marked up, and if so, how much. Request that you be given all receipts for materials.

In most cases, however, it's best to pay a contractor a fixed rate for the whole job; this lets you know exactly what the job will cost, and forces the contractor to plan the work more carefully.

■ *When you meet, give each contractor copies of any documents, worksheets and drawings relating to your project.*

■ *Before signing a contract, make sure you've covered all the details, such as who will be responsible for trash removal.*

Interviewing a General Contractor

If you're looking for a general contractor to manage the entire project, the interview process is slightly different. In the initial meeting, the general contractor will look at your plans or drawings and discuss the scope of the project with you.

Before giving you a price, the general contractor will present your project to subcontractors, each of whom will provide a cost estimate for their portion of the work. After all the subcontractors have submitted their information, the general contractor will total the subcontractor estimates, add his or her own fee (usually a percentage of the total cost), and present you with an itemized rundown and total cost quote.

Because of their knowledge of the construction side of the project, you may want to consult a contractor during the design process. However, to get a firm cost quote, you'll need completed plans.

Playing Detective

Unfortunately, there are some contractors who don't tell the whole truth during interviews. That's why you need to investigate the background of anyone you plan to hire, even if that person has been highly recommended by friends. You don't have to hire a private detective, but take some logical precautions to make sure your contractors are responsible and competent.

First, confirm that each contractor is licensed and insured. Next, check a few of the references at random (not just those given as "good" references). Ask them about the contractor's work quality, whether the schedule was met and how well problems and change orders were handled. Find out if the contractor was available throughout the project and whether he or she listened to the homeowners' concerns. If the contractor has another job in progress, you may ask to visit the site and talk to the homeowner in person.

Talk to local suppliers to see if the contractor has had any credit troubles, and confirm that his or her credit is in good standing. Check with the Better Business Bureau or Chamber of Commerce to see if any complaints have been filed against the contractor. It's not unusual for a reputable, established contractor to have one or two complaints on file—but if you find a pattern of problems, look for someone else.

Other places to check include the local building department and the state contractors license bureau.

Making the Final Choices

Unless there's an obvious first choice, compare the bids and abilities of at least three separate contractors for each position. Many homeowners automatically choose the contractor with the lowest bid, but that's not necessarily a good idea. In fact, you should be wary of any contractor who bids much lower than the competition—something is probably wrong. Price is important, of course, but it's not as important as the contractor's quality of work, level of experience or ability to stay on his or her budget (and the project budget) and on schedule.

If you're managing the project yourself, it's essential that you have a friendly relationship with your contractors, since you'll be in frequent contact with them. If you sense a potential personality conflict, beware. It's perfectly acceptable to disqualify a prospective contractor for that reason alone.

Once you've selected your first choices, double-check to make sure they'll be available when you need them, then arrange another meeting or two to iron out the details and agree on a contract.

Signing a Contract

A contract is a written, signed legal agreement between you and a contractor; it specifies the work to be done, the amount to be paid and the responsibilities of both parties. Contracts protect each of you in case there are misunderstandings during and after construction. Although it's common to hire contractors on the basis of a handshake and verbal promise, it can lead to problems.

Drawing up a contract doesn't need to be complicated. Most remodeling professionals have standard contracts that they use. For a sample contract you can use as a model for your own, see **Worksheet 5** (pages 152-153). You may want to have an attorney check the document before you sign it. A contract for a remodeling project should include:

• *Description of the work.* Include a complete list of the work to be done. Also include your home address—even if plans and specifications documents are attached to the contract.

• *Building permits.* Specify whether you or the contractor will be responsible for getting the necessary permits (see page 76). It's usually best to have the contractor take responsibility for the permits and reviews by the building inspector.

• *Start and completion dates.* State dates clearly and specify what would be considered legitimate grounds for delaying the schedule. Include the time needed for final inspection, and "make-good" time set aside for the contractor to fix any problems. Some contractors will balk at committing to a firm completion date, so it's wise to build some flexibility into the wording of the contract.

• *Price.* Clearly state the specific dollar amount you'll be charged for the work. If the contractor has agreed to a reduced price because you're planning to do some of the work, make sure the contract defines your responsibilities.

• *Payment schedule.* Indicate the amount and the due date of each payment to the contractor. A "good faith" initial down payment of ⅓ to ½ of the total is customary. Another payment is often scheduled about halfway through the project. The final payment should be paid only after the work passes a final inspection. This last payment should be at least 15% of the total; never pay all the money before all the work is completed and approved.

• *Change-order clause.* Make provision for any changes you may order during construction. Change orders may occur simply because you change your mind, or due to unforeseen circumstances discovered during the course of construction. The contract should state the rate at which any extra labor will be charged and the maximum percentage by which the contractor can increase the fees for labor and materials required to make these changes—a markup of 10% to 15% is considered reasonable. In addition, it should specify the changes to the project and resulting charges be summarized in a "change order" and signed by both the homeowner and the contractor.

• *Cleanup.* Specify who is responsible for debris removal and final cleanup.

Optional Clauses

In addition to the essential elements, you may wish to include optional clauses:

• *Holdback clause.* You may want to emphasize that the final payment will be withheld until you've inspected and approved the work. This clause gives you more leverage if you need to motivate the contractor to correct any problems. It's sometimes included in the section that details the payment schedule.

• *List of contractors and suppliers.* If you're working with a general contractor, the contract can list all the anticipated subcontractors and suppliers for the job. Should the general contractor fail to pay these parties, they could have legal claims against you. You should obtain a lien release or waiver from each of them once they're paid in full. **Worksheet 6** (page 154) shows you a sample lien release (also see pages 79-80).

• *Materials substitution.* On larger jobs, architects or general contractors sometimes allow subcontractors to substitute materials so they'll be able to work with their regular suppliers. This clause can specify that subcontractors may not make substitutions for specific materials, such as a particular flooring or countertop product.

• *Delays.* The "acts of nature" clause is designed to pro-

■ *Above: Always back up a handshake agreement with a written contract, even if you know the contractor well.*

tect the contractor from delays caused by natural disasters, strikes and so forth. It can also protect the contractor from delays caused by clients.

• *Warranties.* Labor and materials are generally warrantied by the contractor for a specified period of time, typically one year. Some materials may be warrantied for a longer period by the manufacturer.

• *Contractor's duties.* This clause can stipulate additional responsibilities or pledges to be assumed by the contractor. For example, a contractor can pledge to keep tools and hazardous materials safely locked up and out of the reach of children and pets.

• *Owner's duties.* Some contractors prefer that the contract also lists certain owner responsibilities, such as timely payments, selection of materials and final inspection.

• *Insurance.* On larger jobs, the contract should have a clause stating that each contractor is insured. Insurance against accidental loss due to fire or other disaster is normally provided by your homeowner's insurance. Check your policy to see if such losses are covered; if not, you can take out a short-term policy to cover the project while work is under way.

• *Dispute resolution.* An arbitration clause states that in the event of a dispute, you and the contractor agree to abide by the decision of an impartial third party who will hear both sides of the argument. Arbitration has become an increasingly popular way to avoid court action, mostly because it's much quicker. In most communities, there are services that offer professional arbitration and mediation.

Sample Remodeling Contract (minimal)

Payment Schedule:
Amounts and due dates should be indicated. (Terms may vary between contractors.) Your interim payment is a good time to make sure your contractor is on schedule. Be sure to retain at least 15% (preferably 30%) for the final payment, which will be made only after you're satisfied that the job is truly complete.

Change Orders:
Specify how any changes will be treated. Misunderstandings can be avoided if the contract requires a quote (or a close estimate) in advance for every task not included in the original contract.

Insurance:
Your contractor should carry both Worker's Compensation and liability insurance for all workers used on your project.

Warranties:
Labor and materials are often guaranteed for one year by contractors, but some products and materials may be guaranteed for longer by the manufacturer.

Description of Work:
In addition to a brief verbal description, final drawings and written specifications should be attached to the contract.

Price:
The price should be clearly stated and should be defined as either an estimate or a quote.

Permits:
Is the cost of a building permit included in the price? Or is that the responsibility of the homeowner?

Start and Finish Dates:
List the expected dates, as well as acceptable reasons for delay.

Classic Carpentry Incorporated
222 Oakland Lane
Somewhere, IL 55344

April 14, 2000

John and Jane Smith
4116 Anystreet
Big City, State 12345

Kitchen Remodeling Proposal

Classic Carpentry Inc. (CCI) herein submits a quotation for carpentry labor and building materials (as specified in the attached drawings and specifications) to remodel the kitchen at 4116 Anystreet.

Total Price: **$5, 414.00**

Terms: Initial Payment - $1, 353.50 (25%) upon acceptance of proposal.
Interim Payment - $2,707.00 (50%) upon installation and taping of drywall.
Final Payment - $1,353,50 (25%) upon completion of specified work.

Any changes to this proposal price shall be made in writing, and signed by both CCI and the homeowner. Any price increase shall be agreed upon between the parties before additional work is actually done.

Homeowner agrees to pull and post necessary building permits.

Duration of this project is expected to be five weeks from start to completion. If proposal is accepted by April 17, 2000, and demolition by owner is complete, CCI agrees to begin work on or before Monday, April 27 and expects to be completed by May 29, 2000. CCI shall not be liable for delays due to circumstances beyond its control, including strikes, unavailability of materials, or delays caused by weather.

CCI is licensed, bonded, and insured, and warrants all materials and labor for 24 months following date of completion.

Proposal submitted by:_____Date:_____

Proposal accepted by:_____Date:_____

_____Date:_____

MANAGING THE JOB

A t this point, you've completed most of the major steps of planning for your kitchen remodel. You've polished the plan, set the budget, arranged your finances and hired help as necessary. The next, and final, step is where it all comes together. This is when the dust flies and the walls come crashing down. Even the demolition carries an element of excitement—the old is making way for the new, and soon your new kitchen will become a reality.

Perhaps the greatest challenge of this step is creating a work schedule. If you've assumed the role of general contractor, you'll need to coordinate with all of the subcontractors involved to create a detailed schedule that is efficient but flexible enough to accommodate ordinary delays. This chapter shows you how.

After the work begins, it won't be long before you understand one of the fundamental difficulties with remodeling: the job site is also your home. This means you'll be hosting all the workers and their equipment, as well as the noise and dust they create. To minimize any inconvenience to you and the various tradespeople, make careful preparations to accommodate the work and everyone involved. And be ready to live without your kitchen for a while. Also, as the job progresses, it will be in your best interest to keep all records in order—receipts, contracts, legal documents—to avoid potential problems now and in the future.

■ *Opposite: With careful planning and preparation, the inconvenience of remodeling your kitchen is sure to be forgotten when you see the results.* ■ *Above: To develop an effective schedule, you need to work closely with all your subcontractors.*

The Project Schedule

Scheduling a project requires an understanding of a typical construction sequence. If you're creating the schedule yourself, you'll need to know how to place each subcontractor in the proper order. If you've hired a general contractor, he or she knows how to do this, of course, but you'll certainly be included in the scheduling process. In either case, it's helpful to understand the major steps of the project and what goes into building a schedule. As the start date grows near, make sure you're prepared for the inconveniences of living without your kitchen for the duration of the project.

Creating a Realistic Schedule

Newcomers to scheduling are likely to make some mistakes. One extreme approach to scheduling is to attempt to accomplish the Utopian remodel, in which all the subcontractors complete their tasks in a seamless chain of productivity—without delays. Another approach is less optimistic than the first, but errs by being overly cautious. This is a schedule that's too flexible; it can guarantee the project stays on schedule, but it may take a year or two to complete the job.

An effective, realistic schedule falls between these two extremes. It involves hiring and scheduling all of your subcontractors in advance and building in plenty of slack time at critical points in the schedule, to handle unforeseen delays. Remember that in addition to problems occurring on your project, each of your subcontractors can run into problems with other jobs they are working on at the same time.

If you are acting as the general contractor, be aware that your subcontractors may be inclined to give top priority to another job—for which they are working for a professional general contractor—as the latter has greater promise of repeat business.

The Stages of a Typical Remodeling Project

The timeline presented here is based on a full-scale remodeling job—you can skip any steps that don't apply to your project. These time estimates assume that all the work is being done by professionals. Schedule at least twice as much time for any jobs you plan to do yourself. Also, the estimates given do not account for common delays, such as subcontractors or materials arriving late and inspection delays. And work on a remodeling project often turns up other unpleasant surprises: hidden utilities and water- or insect-damaged structural members are two of the most common. All of these delays and problems can add 20%-40%—sometimes as much as 50%—to a schedule.

■ *1. If your remodeling project includes a room expansion or addition, major construction will be the first phase of the project.*

■ *2. Demolition is the next step. If you decide to do it yourself, be sure to remove all the refuse from the area before the carpenters arrive.*

■ *3. Rough carpentry (constructing or moving walls, framing doors and windows) is done next, usually by a construction carpenter.*

■ *4. The plumber should be the first mechanical contractor—make sure this work is done before the HVAC and electrical contractors arrive.*

1. Major Construction

If your new kitchen involves a room addition, assume that the building contractors will take about four to six weeks to excavate, pour a foundation and erect the shell of the new addition. If your project involves no major structural work, begin with step 2.

2. Demolition

The next task is removing the old cabinets, flooring, countertops and wall surfaces. This work can be done by a general laborer or a subcontractor, or you can do it yourself. Allow 2 to 4 days for this stage of the project.

3. Rough Carpentry

The next step involves building walls, framing new doors and windows and adding beams and partitions. This work will be done by a carpenter, or by a crew of carpenters employed by your general contractor. Allow 1 to 2 weeks for this work, depending on the size of the job. Carpenters will return to complete the finish phases of the project later.

4. Plumbing

The plumber should arrive to "rough-in" the new supply and drain, waste and vent pipes after the carpenters are finished. Allow 2 to 4 days for this stage. The plumber will return after the cabinets and counters are installed to set and hook up the sink, faucets, garbage disposal and water-fed appliances.

5. HVAC

Schedule your HVAC (heating, ventilation, air-conditioning) contractor or boiler contractor after the plumbing and before the electrical work. Depending on the extent of the job, allow 1 to 4 days for this work.

6. Electrical

Before the walls are insulated and finished, the electrician needs to run new cable and install outlet boxes. If the electrical installation isn't very complicated, allow 1 to 2 days for this job, but if a new subpanel or upgraded service is needed, allow 3-5 days. The electrician will return to connect the outlets, lights and appliances after the walls are finished and the cabinets are installed.

7. Wall Finishes

Allow 1 to 2 weeks for insulating walls, installing, taping and finishing the drywall and painting or wallpapering. There may be several different subcontractors involved. Typically, a carpenter or insulation subcontractor will insulate the walls, a two-person crew will hang the drywall, a taper will finish the seams; a third crew will paint

■ 5. HVAC (heating, ventilation, air-conditioning) work, if necessary, should be completed before the electrical installation begins.

■ 6. Electrical work is next. Plumbing, HVAC and electrical work must pass inspection before the walls are insulated and finished.

■ 7. Finish the walls and ceilings before installing the flooring and cabinets. This work may require several different subcontractors.

■ 8. Flooring is usually laid before the cabinets are installed; the work is easier at this time and your new cabinets won't be damaged.

■ *9. Install the cabinets next. Stock cabinets are installed by a carpenter, custom cabinets by the contractor who built them.*

■ *10. Install the countertops. Laminate countertops may be installed by a carpenter, other materials by specialty contractors.*

■ *11. Schedule finish carpentry (wood trim, baseboards and window and door casings) near the end of the project.*

■ *12. Installation of appliances and plumbing and electrical fixtures is the last step. This work is usually done by your plumber and electrician.*

or wallpaper the walls. Painting and wallpapering can be done before or after the flooring and cabinets are installed.

8. Flooring

It can take 1 to 4 days to install flooring, depending on the material, the size of the room and the condition of the subfloor. Flooring contractors generally prefer to work before the cabinetry is in place.

9. Cabinets

Stock and semi-custom cabinets are usually installed by a carpenter, while custom cabinets are typically installed by the professionals who built them. For a typical kitchen, allow 1 to 3 days for cabinet installation.

10. Countertops

Laminate countertops are sometimes installed by a carpenter, while ceramic tile, solid-surface, stone and stainless steel countertops are almost always installed by contractors who specialize in the material. Allow 1 to 3 days for countertop installation.

11. Finish Carpentry

Window moldings, baseboards and other trim are installed by a carpenter. This may be the same carpenter who did the rough framing work or it may be a finish carpenter who specializes in this kind of precision work. Allow 2 to 4 days in your schedule for finish carpentry.

12. Fixtures and Appliances

Sinks, faucets, light fixtures and appliances may be installed by a carpenter, plumber, electrician or retailer— or you can do this work yourself. Although none of these individual jobs takes much time, there may be many people involved, so it's best to allow 3 to 5 days for this stage of the process.

13. Your Inspection

No kitchen remodeling project is complete until you've inspected the work and had any problems corrected. This final inspection is your responsibility, and fixing the problems you discover is the responsibility of the contractor who did the work. Allow at least 2 weeks in your schedule to have any problems you've found in your final inspection resolved by the appropriate contractors.

Developing a Schedule

The key to creating a successful remodeling schedule is to develop a realistic timeline. You can use blank planning calendar pages (available in office supply stores) to draw up your master schedule. Here's how to proceed:

1. Order all the materials needed for your project and

record when each one is scheduled to arrive. Nothing can ruin a schedule more quickly than leaving tradespeople waiting for materials.

2. Call each of your subcontractors and ask them to estimate the time they'll need to complete each phase of their job. Be sure to tell them that you're simply trying to schedule the project; your subcontractors may become uncooperative if they think you're trying to get them to commit to a specific deadline.

3. Create a detailed master schedule that includes the starting and ending dates of each task. Be especially liberal when scheduling any work you're planning to do yourself.

Allow at least ½ day of down time between subcontractors, and don't schedule any to start work on a Friday. On your schedule, mark these blank periods "cleanup"—though these are just a buffer in case something goes over schedule.

Include the names and telephone numbers of all your subcontractors and materials suppliers on the schedule, and the dates of all deliveries. Finally, make reminder notes and reserve some time for each required inspection (see **Getting Permits**, page 76).

4. Invite all your subcontractors to a brief meeting, and give them a copy of your master schedule. Ask each to confirm the dates on the schedule. If any scheduling conflicts arise, try to resolve these issues while everyone is present.

If a subcontractor asks for a change in the schedule, be firm but not inflexible. It's better to stretch out your project than to force an overworked and irritated contractor to meet a tight deadline. Keep in mind, though, that stretching the schedule for one subcontractor may make it difficult for others to finish their work on time.

5. Once the project is under way, call to confirm with each subcontractor shortly before he or she is scheduled to arrive. Also call to confirm all scheduled deliveries.

■ *A detailed master calendar is essential for keeping the job on schedule.*

Getting Permits

In most communities, a major remodeling project requires a general permit from the city building inspections office. Your general contractor (or you) will apply for a building permit. Permits for the plumber, electrician and HVAC contractor may be included with the general permit or they may be separate permits. You'll pay for the permit either directly or as part of the contractor's bill. The fee is usually a percentage of the total cost of the project.

If your new kitchen includes a room addition, you may also need to present your plans to your city zoning office when you apply for the building permit.

If you're planning to do any of the electrical, plumbing, heating or ventilation work yourself, you'll need to get the permit. In this case, the inspector will want to see detailed plans of your proposed changes, and he or she may question you carefully to make sure you're competent to do the work.

All building and mechanical permits require an on-site review by an inspector. When you apply for the permit, the inspector will explain the on-site inspection schedule. For mechanical systems, such as plumbing and wiring, inspectors will want to inspect the work while the wires and pipes are still visible, before the wall surfaces are installed.

Be sure to add time to your schedule for inspections. After calling for an inspection, it's not uncommon to wait half a day or more for an inspector to arrive. Ask the inspections office how much lead time they typically need to respond to a call. And most importantly, make sure all the necessary work is complete; an inspection failure not only halts a project, it also adds extra time to correct the problem that caused the failure.

After you pass the final inspection, you will be issued a *Certificate of Occupancy* (C.O.). This document is necessary for such things as obtaining loans and for verifying that your remodel was approved by the local building department, should you ever sell your house.

Living Through It

Be prepared for the fact that remodeling your kitchen will be a major inconvenience. For several weeks, or even months, you won't be able to cook or eat in your kitchen—and other rooms in your home may need to be turned into temporary storage areas for appliances, cabinets and other materials.

The best approach is to plan as carefully as you can, then grin and bear it. Eat out whenever possible; get yourself invited to dinner as often as you can manage. If possible, set up a temporary kitchen near a faucet in the garage or basement. Use folding tables and old countertops as food preparation and serving areas. For cooking, use a microwave oven, electric hotplate or crockpot; just be careful of fire danger. . Use the laundry tub for washing dishes, and don't hesitate to rely on paper plates, plastic flatware and prepared foods.

Although remodeling projects typically generate a lot of dust and mess, there are ways to keep it from spreading. Before work begins, isolate the work area from the rest of the house with sheets of 4-mil plastic, sealing the edges with tape. For maximum dust containment, every entrance to the work area should have a double air-lock—two separate walls of plastic that have a slit to walk through and a taut sheet of plastic overlapping the slit. Close the heating and air conditioning ducts in the work area, and seal them with plastic to keep dust from circulating through the house. Keep the interior doors closed, and cover the floors with sheets of thin hardboard that are taped together.

Here are more tips that can help you survive a remodeling project:

• Rent a roll-off trash dumpster, or rent or borrow a

■ *Before work begins, seal the work area and heating ducts with plastic to keep construction dust from spreading.*

pickup truck. In some communities, there are special provisions for city workers to pick up and dispose of building materials.

• Designate a trash area. If possible, locate it near a convenient window through which debris can be shoveled.

• Protect your shrubs and siding with plywood. If you'll be doing the demolition and cleanup yourself, make sure you have a sturdy wheelbarrow.

• Set aside a space where your subcontractors can store their tools and materials—in your garage or basement, or in a room next to the kitchen.

• Make room in the garage for a cutting area for tradespeople, to minimize noise and dust in your home. In winter, rent a space heater to keep the area warm, but be careful of fire and exhaust hazards.

• Designate a service door for workers to use.

• Protect the floors and hallways between the service door and the work area by laying down sheets of thin cardboard taped together.

• Provide window fans to ventilate the work area when demolition, sanding, painting or staining is under way.

• Use any down time in the schedule to catch up on paperwork and phone calls and clean up the work site.

■ *A convenient window can serve as a chute for moving construction debris out of the work area; use sheets of plywood to protect your shrubs and siding*

The Project Details

Regardless of who is managing the project, it's important that you do your part to help the job go smoothly. This may include preparing your house for when the workers arrive, checking deliveries, getting permits and calling for inspections, staying in contact with contractors and keeping track of all the receipts and legal documents. Making payments is certainly among your responsibilities, although you'll want to make sure everything is in order before pulling out your checkbook.

Project Management

If you're managing the project yourself, subcontractors and laborers will expect you to act as your own general contractor. This typically means that you'll need to be available, either in person or by phone, to answer questions and make decisions on the spot. You'll also need to keep track of delivery dates for materials, make phone calls, run occasional errands and keep track of all the paperwork.

You'll also need to provide a way for workers to access

the house when you aren't home. One solution is a lock-box—a security-coded box that contains a house key and can be hung on the doorknob. Remind your contractors to lock the house and return the key to the lockbox when they're done.

Many homeowners find it helpful to take time off from their jobs while a remodeling project is under way. Another option is to work an earlier or later shift so you can be home while the contractors are working.

Preparation

As the starting day for your project draws near, make sure you've taken care of the following details:

• Check over all your contracts once more, and make sure they've all been signed.

• Call all your subcontractors to confirm their starting dates and make sure their insurance is up to date. While you're on the phone, ask if there's any preparation you can do to make sure their work goes smoothly.

• Confirm that your homeowner's insurance is up to date and that you're covered for any loss due to fire or accidents while the work is under way.

• Make sure your financing is in place and that the funds will be available when you need to pay your sub-contractors and suppliers.

• Make sure your alternate kitchen area is ready to use while the remodeling project is under way.

Deliveries

Big remodeling projects involve the delivery of large quantities of materials. If you've hired a general contractor, he or she will arrange the delivery of these materials and make sure all delivered goods are correct and in good condition. If you're acting as your own general contractor, these will be your responsibilities. You also have the option of picking up some of the materials yourself, to save the cost of delivery charges, but this requires extra time and access to a pickup truck.

You'll also need a place to store your materials and keep them safe until you need them—you don't want to have your new appliances stolen out of an unlocked garage. For any materials you don't pick up yourself, make sure to be present during the scheduled delivery to confirm that everything is complete and correct.

It's crucial that you carefully inspect all shipments for damage and to check them against the invoice for any missing materials. Delivery drivers are almost always in a hurry and may thrust the invoice under your nose for a signature the instant they arrive. Don't cave in to this pressure; always take the time to review the list of items and inspect the contents before you sign. It can be helpful to call the dispatcher's office a few days before the delivery and let them know you'll need to delay the driver for a few minutes while you review the shipment.

If you find any missing or damaged items, don't sign the paperwork and don't accept the delivery. Call the supplier immediately and arrange to have the problem corrected. If there's a significant problem with the shipment, ask for a written response that spells out the supplier's obligations.

■ *It's essential that you or your general contractor carefully inspect all deliveries before you sign for them.*

Keeping Records

A big remodeling project can generate dozens, if not hundreds, of pieces of paper—receipts, invoices, delivery slips, permits and contracts. Keeping accurate records can be crucial to avoiding legal disputes and tax problems, so make sure you have a safe place to store these documents and a good system for organizing them. If you don't already have a fireproof file box, this is a good time to buy one. A folder with several divider pockets will come in handy when sorting receipts.

If you're working with a general contractor, most of the records related to the actual job will be the contractor's responsibility. However, it's important that you keep contracts you have signed and records of any payments made to the general contractor.

If you're managing the job yourself, keep a ledger and record on it every expenditure related to the project, but especially materials and labor. Include the dates and methods of payment. When your cleared checks return from the bank, store them with your remodeling records.

■ *Keep your remodeling contracts, receipts and other important papers in a fireproof lock box.*

Change Orders

Resist the impulse to change your mind once the project is under way. An alteration to an approved remodeling plan is known as a "change order," and these orders always cost money—sometimes a lot of money. Changing your plan creates added expense for contractors who've agreed to a tight schedule and a clear work plan, so they're well within their rights to charge you more for those changes.

It's not uncommon for a contractor who has underbid the job to try to boost his or her profits by overcharging for a change order. However, if you've followed the suggestions for hiring professionals, your contract will specify limits on what can be charged.

Making Payments

The contracts you've signed with contractors should include a payment schedule. Payment schedules vary widely, but in most cases you'll be making an initial down payment to each contractor and paying the balance upon completion of the work. For smaller jobs you can expect to pay 30% to 50% up front and the balance when the work is completed, although some states limit the initial payment to as little as 10%. For larger projects, you should pay only 10% to 20% up front, with the

balance due at specified intervals during construction.

Always arrange to withhold at least 15% of the total fee until the work is completed; this gives contractors an incentive to finish the work on time and fix any problems that come up. Even if you have the utmost faith in your contractors, never make final payment until they've completed all the work to your satisfaction. Also, make sure to get itemized receipts for all your payments.

Mechanic's Liens & Releases

A mechanic's lien is a legal claim on your property by a contractor or supplier who hasn't been paid according to a legal agreement. Any licensed general contractor, subcontractor or supplier who's involved in the improvement of your property can file a lien if they aren't paid. It makes no difference whether it's you or your general contractor who failed to make the payment—the lien will still be filed against your property.

Liens are rare, but if you find yourself on the receiving end, it can make your life pretty miserable. If you try to sell your house, for example, even years later, an outstanding lien can make it impossible to close the deal.

If you've planned correctly, the contracts you've signed

with your contractors will clearly state the payment schedule and the responsibility of the contractor and the homeowner, making a lien unlikely. However, in some cases, your receipts will be the only proof that you've paid for the materials and labor.

Before making the final payment to any contractor, always get a lien release. A lien release, or waiver, is a legal document that confirms that the contractor has finished the work and has been paid in full for those services. If you're using a general contractor, make sure you get lien releases from all subcontractors, as well as a final lien release from the general contractor before you make the final payment. **Worksheet 6** (page 154) shows a sample lien release you can use as a model.

If a contractor intends to file a lien, the law requires that first you be notified in writing. After informing you, the contractor is then allowed to file a lien with the county recorder, and must send a copy of the document to you. If you find yourself served with a lien, here is what you should do:

1. First, determine if the claim is legitimate. Get out your receipts and canceled checks, and compare them against the contracts and invoices. If you have not paid money that's rightfully owed, honor the commitment and pay the lienholder as soon as possible. Even if it's your general contractor, not you, who has failed to make payments, you should still pay the subcontractor. Later, you can legally deduct this sum from the final payment you owe the general contractor.

2. If, for some reason, you can't pay the money in dispute, or if you believe the lien has no merit, schedule a meeting with the contractor and try to work out an agreement. In some cases, correcting a simple bookkeeping error can resolve the misunderstanding. If you have deliberately withheld final payment because of unresolved problems with the contractor's work, point this out and offer the contractor a chance to make good on the contract in exchange for your final payment.

3. If a private meeting doesn't resolve your differences, suggest that the case be referred to a professional arbitrator (if your contract doesn't already have an arbitration clause). Professional arbitrators are familiar with these kinds of disputes, and their decisions are binding. Arbitration is almost always faster and cheaper than a court case.

4. If all attempts to settle the dispute fail, you can wait for the suit to be filed and plead your case before a judge. Just make sure you have copies of all contracts and receipts before you head into court. If the sum in dispute is under a few thousand dollars, the case may be heard in small claims court, in which case you and the contractor can present your cases without lawyers. If the

■ *Many problems can be avoided by staying in close touch with your contractors throughout the project.*

■ *If you decide to act as your own general contractor, all your subcontractors will need to be able to reach you by phone during the day.*

sum in dispute is larger, however, you'll need to hire an attorney to represent you.

Taxes

A remodeling project can affect your tax burden in several ways—some good, some not so good. The tax laws are always changing, however, and you'll need to consult a tax professional to get up-to-date tax information that applies to your situation.

Property Tax

If your new kitchen adds substantial market value to your home, your city or county tax assessor may raise the estimated value of your home, and you'll end up paying more in property taxes. Small projects that don't alter the floor plan of your home will probably be ignored by the tax assessor.

Income Tax

If you've financed the project with a home improvement or home equity loan or a second mortgage, the interest on that loan is probably deductible on your income tax. This applies only to the interest on loans secured by your home. Most taxpayers can't take a direct deduction on the cost of the remodeling project. However, if you take a deduction for a home office, you may qualify for a deduction; check with a tax professional.

Capital Gains Tax

If you ever decide to sell your home and move into a property of lesser value, you'll be subject to capital gains tax on the net profit you gained from the sale. However, you may be able to use the amount you invested in

remodeling to reduce this net profit.

For example, if your present home originally cost $100,000 and you sell it for $160,000, you'd be subject to capital gains tax on the $60,000 that you made on the sale. However, if you've spent $50,000 on a new kitchen, and you have the documents to prove it, you can add this amount to your original purchase price to increase the cost basis of your house. For tax purposes, then, your capital gain on the sale would be just $10,000.

Bear in mind, however, that some remodeling expenses can't be used to increase your home's cost basis. Repair and maintenance work, for example, isn't considered a capital improvement. The cost of buying and installing new cabinets would be a capital improvement, but the cost of repainting or refacing your old cabinets wouldn't.

TIP

Payment Tips

Never make your final payment until you've inspected the work—even if the contractor is a good friend. Your contract should specify a final payment that's at least 15% (and preferably 30% to 35%) of the total amount due to the contractor. This is your only leverage for ensuring that the contractor finishes the job to your satisfaction. Once you've inspected the work and are satis-

fied with the results, be sure to get a signed lien release when you hand over the final check.

Some contractors are masters at talking homeowners into paying earlier than the contract stipulates. Don't give in to this; under no circumstances should you pay in full before all the work is completed.

CABINETS, COUNTERS & SINKS

New cabinets and countertops typically reflect the most significant investments in a kitchen remodeling project. In addition to their high costs, often totaling as much as 50% of the project cost, the cabinets and countertops play a decisive role in determining the look and feel of a kitchen.

The choice to replace the cabinets usually defines the line between a cosmetic make-over and a major remodeling job; if you're replacing cabinets, you're likely to replace counter-tops, appliances and perhaps the flooring. If your present cabinets provide adequate storage, you may consider refacing or painting them—either option is far less costly than installing new cabinets.

As for countertop materials, you'll find there are many to choose from—including less common options, such as wood, natural stone, stainless steel and concrete. However, most homeowners select one of the three surfaces discussed in this chapter—plastic laminate, ceramic tile and solid surfacing. Be sure to consider the advantages and disadvantages of each countertop material, and remember that you aren't limited to one; you may use a plastic laminate surface for most of your counters, for example, then splurge for a small section of butcher block or marble.

Compared with cabinets and countertops, the sink and faucet comprise a relatively small part of your kitchen remodeling budget, but the importance of these purchases far out-weighs their costs, since they are typically the most-used elements of the kitchen. Sinks and faucets come in wide ranges of designs and configurations, which should make it easy to find ones that fit your budget, lifestyle and design scheme.

■ *Opposite: Coordinating your cabinets and countertops can have dramatic results. In this kitchen, the decorative edge along the countertops complements the bold lines of the cabinetry.* ■ *Above: Today's sink and faucet designs allow you to create any effect you desire, including the old-fashioned look of this apron-front porcelain sink and antique-style faucet and sprayer.*

Kitchen Cabinets

If it's been a while since you last shopped for kitchen cabinets, you may be pleasantly surprised to discover that many styles and features that previously were offered only with custom cabinets are now standard in more affordable lines. If you've never shopped for cabinets before, you may be surprised simply by how many options there are.

You can buy cabinets at home centers, cabinet showrooms and custom cabinet shops. If you're working with a kitchen designer, he or she will help you with every step of your cabinet purchase. Many home centers and showrooms also have designers on staff who can assist you as well. A general contractor may help you buy cabinets or refer you to a reputable designer or showroom. In any case, you'll want to be familiar with cabinet construction and know how to spot a quality product.

The Three Grades of Cabinets

Kitchen cabinets are generally divided into three grades,

based on how they are constructed. To some extent, the grades indicate quality, but not very accurately. The best test of quality is a thorough physical inspection (see page 87).

• *Stock cabinets* are factory-made to standard sizes and are typically sold off-the-shelf in home centers. Widths range from 9 in. to 48 in., in 3 in. increments. Stock cabinets are the least expensive of the three grades, but they offer the fewest design options. While the quality is generally lower, a well-made stock cabinet can be a very good value. If your stock cabinets have to be ordered, it may be a couple of days to a couple of weeks before they arrive.

• *Semi-custom cabinets* are also factory-made to standard sizes, but they offer far more options of finish, size, features and materials than stock cabinets. These are typically sold in showrooms, and are priced between stock and custom cabinets. Semi-custom are the best

■ *This kitchen showcases several recent design trends: color accents, architectural molding and focal-point cabinets.*

choice for homeowners who want better-quality cabinets with some special features but don't want to pay the high prices for a custom product. You should allow 3 to 8 weeks lead time when ordering semi-custom cabinets.

• *Custom cabinets* offer the most in both quality and available options. Each unit is custom-built to fit your kitchen. It's wise to shop around before settling on a custom cabinetmaker, as prices can vary widely. If you choose to have your cabinets custom-made, expect a lead time of about 6 to 10 weeks.

Selecting a Cabinet Type

Cabinets are available in two types: *face-frame*, and *frameless*, or "Euro-style." Face-frame cabinets have frames around the front of the cabinet box, or *carcass*, made of solid hardwood. The doors on face-frame cabinets mount over the frame, and the hinges are exposed. Face-frame cabinets typically have a more traditional look.

Frameless cabinets have no face-frame and the doors span the entire width of the carcass. The doors are mounted using *cup* hinges, which are invisible when the

doors are closed. The plainer, cleaner styling of frameless cabinets gives them a contemporary look.

There are no distinct advantages or disadvantages between the two cabinet types. However, by virtue of not having a face frame, frameless cabinets offer slightly more storage space than framed types, and their drawers are a bit wider, for the same reason.

Recognizing Quality

To be sure you're getting your money's worth with your cabinet purchase, inspect all the major components:

Basic Materials

Most cabinet carcasses are made with plywood or particle board. Plywood is stronger than particle board of the same thickness but that doesn't mean you should avoid the latter. If the cabinet is made with particle board, make sure the board used is $5/8$-in. to $3/4$-in. thick. It should also have a vinyl or melamine coating on the inside surfaces, to protect it from water damage. Most frameless cabinets (including the doors) are made

---

TIP

Quality Standards

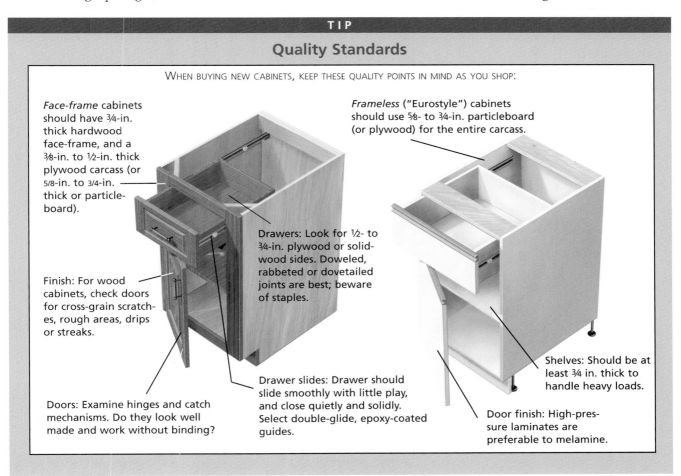

WHEN BUYING NEW CABINETS, KEEP THESE QUALITY POINTS IN MIND AS YOU SHOP:

Face-frame cabinets should have ¾-in. thick hardwood face-frame, and a ⅜-in. to ½-in. thick plywood carcass (or 5/8-in. to 3/4-in. thick or particleboard).

Finish: For wood cabinets, check doors for cross-grain scratches, rough areas, drips or streaks.

Doors: Examine hinges and catch mechanisms. Do they look well made and work without binding?

Drawers: Look for ½- to ¾-in. plywood or solid-wood sides. Doweled, rabbeted or dovetailed joints are best; beware of staples.

Drawer slides: Drawer should slide smoothly with little play, and close quietly and solidly. Select double-glide, epoxy-coated guides.

Frameless ("Eurostyle") cabinets should use ⅝- to ¾-in. particleboard (or plywood) for the entire carcass.

Shelves: Should be at least ¾ in. thick to handle heavy loads.

Door finish: High-pressure laminates are preferable to melamine.

with particle board.

On cabinets with natural wood surfaces, pay close attention to how well the grain and colors of the different pieces match.

Drawers

A drawer is a good indicator of a cabinet's quality. Better drawers are made with plywood or solid wood and their pieces are assembled with strong joints, such as dovetail, dowel or rabbet joints. Avoid drawers that were put together with staples. Also, four-sided drawers, with the drawer front attached to the front side, are stronger and more durable than those with three sides that use the drawer front as the fourth side.

Drawer slides should be smooth and sound and allow little play from side to side. You can also check the slide's load rating, which should be at least 75 pounds.

Doors

If the rest of the cabinet is of a suitable quality, the doors should be fine, and your decision will be based largely on appearance. But cabinet doors receive a lot of use, and they need a durable finish to protect them over the years. Flat, particle-board doors, which are commonly found on frameless cabinets, may be faced with a plastic laminate similar to the material used on countertops. This is a durable, washable material that should last a very long time; just make sure the facing is laminate and not just a coating of melamine—a much less durable finish.

If you're looking for wood doors with a stain or a clear finish, make sure the outer wood veneers look good and the blending of the grain and color variations is attractive. Examine the finish for common flaws, such as inconsistency, rough areas, drips or cross-grain sanding marks. You may have specific reasons for choosing pine or another softwood, but remember that hardwoods, such as maple, oak and cherry, are more durable.

An alternative to the traditional raised-panel wood door is the vinyl-clad door. Made from medium-density fiberboard (MDF) with a tough vinyl "foil," vinyl-clad doors look like painted wood doors but have a more durable finish. Another advantage is that vinyl-clad doors expand and contract less than wood doors, so there's less risk of the paint cracking along the edges of the panel.

Adding Cabinet Features

There are many new accessories designed to help you squeeze more storage space from your cabinets. They include tiered lazy Susans hidden behind 90-degree folding doors, shelves that pull and swivel outward to make use of blind-corner space and 3-in.-wide pantry units that put dead filler space to work. (For more

■ *The glass cabinet doors in this kitchen feature a crisscrossing flute pattern that lets in light but obscures the contents of the cupboards.*

information on time-saving cabinet features, see **Choosing Cabinets,** pages 24-25.)

When selecting your new cabinets, you may want to consider some of the following add-ons. Even if you end up sticking with the basics, you'll have a good idea of all the new options. A recent trend in traditionally styled kitchens is using cabinets that are styled like furniture,

■ *Shallow drawers under the sink can provide a convenient spot for supplies and recycling bins.*

including accessories such as galley rails, fluted-pilaster fillers and furniture feet. Many classic molding patterns, such as rope, egg-and-dart, dentil and spindle-rail, have found their way onto cabinets, and valance segments, such as arches, frets and scallops, are being used to bridge cabinet runs where they break at windows.

Wall cabinets are no longer automatically placed in a straight, uninterrupted run of like-size cases. They're often staggered at different heights, sometimes with a unit hung alone, to provide a casual, unfitted look. Open shelves and plate racks are another way to break up the horizontal lines of the cabinetry.

Base cabinets are also breaking away from a uniform height, as hutches, baking centers and other specialized units become more popular. These varying counter heights allow you to customize the height of your kitchen's work and storage areas (see **User-Friendly Kitchens,** pages 28-29). You can use coordinated transition pieces, such as built-in cutting boards or knife storage units, to cover the transition between cabinets of different heights.

If you like glass cabinet doors, remember that not everything stored in the kitchen is worthy of display. Frosted panes or a textured pattern can obscure the view through the glass without ruining the effect. Another option is to include glass doors on the few cabinets that hold your fine china and glassware and use solid fronts on the cabinets that hold your everyday items.

SOURCES

Kitchen Cabinets

ARISTOKRAFT: 812/482-2527; www.aristokraft.com
CANAC KITCHENS: 800/226-2248; www.kohlerco.com
DECORA: 812/634-2288; decoracabinets.com
HOME CREST: 219/533-9571, www.homecrestcab.com
IKEA: 800/434-4532; www.ikea.com
KRAFTMAID: 800/571-1990; www.kraftmaid.com
MASTERCRAFT: 800/527-2381; www.mcraft.com
MEDALLION KITCHENS: 612/442-5171; www.medallioncabinetry.com
MERILLAT: 800/575-8763; www.merillat.com
PLAIN & FANCY: 800/447-9006; www.homeportfolio.com
RUTT CUSTOM CABINETRY: 800/420-7888; www.rutt1.com
SIEMATIC: 800/765-5266; www.siematic.com
STARMARK: 800/959-5990; www.starmarkcabinetry.com
TIMBERLAKE: 800/895-8391; www.timberlake.com
WELLBORN: 800/762-4475; www.wellborncabinet.com
WOOD-MODE: 570/374-2711; www.woodmode.com
YESTERTEC DESIGN: 610/838-1194; www.yestertec.com
YORKTOWNE: 800/777-0065; www.yorktowneinc.com

■ *Customized base cabinets can hide surprises, such as this freewheeling serving cart or a narrow pull-out spice pantry that fits between two standard base cabinets.*

■ *Laminate countertops are available in a wide range of patterns and colors, including many that mimic the look of more costly materials.*

Home centers and kitchen dealers typically display an array of laminate counter samples on pegboards, which allows you to view many styles and options at a glance.

Choosing Color & Pattern

The current trend in counter colors is to use deep, rich hues inspired by nature. If you're hesitant to use a bold color everywhere, you might use a neutral color for the counter and a bright accent color for the backsplash that picks up one of the counter colors or a contrasting color. You can also use the edge of the counter as an accent by adding a contrasting strip or a different material.

Most laminate colors are available in a variety of sheens. For a hard-working family kitchen, it's best to select a tough, easy-to-clean matte finish. If you're attracted to a shiny finish, keep in mind that it will show wear more easily and be more difficult to keep clean. For the same reasons, deeply textured finishes are less desirable, especially for work areas.

Once you've narrowed down your choices, make sure the samples work with your new cabinets, floors and appliances. Take the samples home and place them on your counters for a day or two to see how they look under different lighting conditions. Some manufacturers even match their laminate countertops with laminate facings for cabinet doors.

Ensuring Quality

The easiest and cheapest way to buy a laminate countertop is to pick one out at a home center. The ready-made counters you'll find there are typically *post-*

Laminate Countertops

These days, laminate countertops have an undeserved reputation as the stuff you settle for if you can't afford solid-surfacing or natural stone. It's true that at just $15 to $50 per linear foot, even a good laminate is easy on your budget, but laminates have far more going for them than price. They're hard-wearing and durable; a properly installed and cared for laminate countertop should last at least 10 to 15 years.

Plastic laminate is formed from layers of resin-saturated paper that are bonded under pressure, then given a protective coating of clear melamine. The laminate is glued to particle board to create the countertop. Since the top layer of paper—know as the *photo* layer—can depict anything, laminates are available in hundreds of colors and patterns. Laminate countertops also can be manufactured with a variety of edge treatments.

An alternative to standard laminate is *color-through* laminate, in which the surface color runs all the way through the sheet. The advantages of this product are that it doesn't have the dark edge that standard laminate has and surface damage may be less noticeable; the disadvantage is that it costs about three times as much as standard laminate.

SOURCES
Laminate Countertops

FORMICA: 800/367-6422; www.formica.com
LAMINART: 800/323-7624; www.laminart.com
NEVAMAR: 800/638-4380; www.nevamar.com
PIONITE: 800/777-9112; www.pionite.com
WILSONART: 800/433-3222; www.wilsonart.com

■ *Curved laminate surfaces can add a custom look without breaking your budget.*

formed—this means that the backsplash, counter and rounded front apron are all formed from one piece. Although ready-made countertops cost the least (about $15 per linear foot), your selection is usually limited to a few colors and styles. In addition, the thin laminate used for post-forming doesn't have the impact resistance that general-purpose laminate has. Also, you'll need to cut the finished counter to fit your kitchen; on an exposed end, this will leave an unfinished edge.

You can also order a counter directly from a fabricator or through a home center, kitchen dealer or kitchen designer. Be sure to have the fabricator come to your house to measure your kitchen. Most fabricators will also deliver the finished countertops and install them. Whether you choose this option or not, carefully inspect the countertops before the installation, checking the following points:

• The laminate should be bonded to a substrate of particle board or medium-density fiberboard (MDF), which doesn't have voids like some ply-wood.

• The laminate should be fully bonded to this substrate. It's easy to check the edges; in the center, tap the surface; it should sound solid, not hollow.

• There should be absolutely no flaws on any visible surface; laminate cannot be repaired.

Before installation, make sure that the supporting cabinets are level. If they aren't, they must be shimmed before the countertop is installed. After installation, inspect the finished countertop. The seams should be tight, with no obvious gaps. The corner seams should meet at a 45° angle and be both glued and mechanically fastened. Other than the corners, there should be only

two seams, at the backsplash and the front edge. The laminate along the ends and edges should be securely bonded, and the backsplash should fit tightly to the countertop and the wall. Any gaps and seams should be caulked to create a watertight seal.

To keep your laminate countertop looking like new, follow the manufacturer's directions. Avoid scouring pads and cleansers, use a cutting board for chopping and slicing, and place hot pots and pans on trivets, never directly on the counter.

TIP
Laminate Edge Options

YOUR OPTIONS FOR STANDARD LAMINATE EDGES INCLUDE: A. SELF-EDGE; B. WATERFALL EDGE; C. NO-DRIP EDGE.

YOUR OPTIONS FOR CUSTOM LAMINATE EDGES INCLUDE: D. ACCENT-COLOR EDGE; E. ROUNDED WOOD EDGE.

Ceramic Tile Countertops

Ceramic tile is a popular choice for countertops and backsplashes for a few good reasons. It's available in a vast range of sizes, styles and colors; it's durable and can be repaired; and some tile—not all—is reasonably priced. Tile is also relatively easy to install, and many homeowners learn how to do it themselves to create a truly custom look.

As with all other kitchen materials, however, tile has its disadvantages. One is that tile doesn't create a perfectly smooth or flat surface, making it a poor surface for some tasks, such as rolling dough, and also making wiping the counters more difficult. Another potential drawback is that the grout that seals the spaces between individual tiles is prone to staining, but much of that is preventable. Tile is also a very hard surface that's unforgiving when you drop a glass or baking dish.

Understanding Tile & Grout

Ceramic tiles are made of fired clay; the longer and hot-

ter they're fired, the harder and denser they get. For countertops, use only *glazed* ceramic tile. The glaze is a hard, glass-like coating that protects the top surface from moisture and stains and adds strength to the tile.

Ceramic tile is rated 1 through 5 for hardness, which translates to durability. Class 1 includes most wall tile, while Class 5 is rated for heavy-duty commercial floors. Most tile dealers will simply recommend floor tile for countertops. "Commercial" tile includes Class 3, 4 or 5; any of these is suitable for countertops.

While glazing protects the tile surface from most types of stains, the grout is still vulnerable because it's so porous, but there are effective ways to minimize this risk. If you're installing your own tile, use a grout that contains a latex additive, or mix the grout powder with a liquid latex additive instead of water; both will add stain-resistance. And always seal the grout with a high-quality grout sealer (be sure it's safe for food contact). New grout should be sealed after it fully cures, then again about once a year after that.

If you're hiring professionals to install your tile,

request that they use an epoxy grout, which is much less absorptive than standard grout and doesn't have to be sealed. Because epoxy grout can be difficult to work with, it's not recommended for beginning tile-setters.

The staff at a good tile store can tell you all you need to know about tile and grout; just make sure to tell them where you're using the tile and who is going to install it.

Installing Tile

Tiling a countertop is within the skills range of most do-it-yourselfers, but there are some impor-

■ *The different-colored tiles in this countertop create a charming checkerboard effect.*

tant preparations to make before you get to the fun part of laying the tiles. A typical tile countertop starts with ³/₄-in. thick exterior-grade plywood, followed by a cementitious backer board, ¹/₄-in. to ¹/₂-in. thick. The backer board won't be damaged by any water that gets through the tile. A professional installation may include a thick layer of mortar instead of backer board, but that installation is too advanced for most amateurs. The tile is secured to the backer board with a latex-fortified *thin-set* adhesive. When the adhesive dries, the grout is applied to complete the installation.

If you're planning to build and tile your own countertop, it will be worth it to buy a do-it-yourself book devoted to the subject. You can also contact the Tile Council of America (see page 155) and request their latest tile installation manual.

Choosing Tile

Ceramic tile is available in many types, colors, patterns and sizes, and the prices can vary widely. However, there's an incredible variety available for less than $10 per square foot installed (by a professional)—and you can make clever, unique designs out of basic tile for half that amount. The following are a few of the basic criteria you'll consider when selecting tile.

Color

Since solid colors are the least costly, you can customize your countertop inexpensively by creating a field of solid-color tiles and using specialty tiles as an accent. In general, keep countertops fairly simple, as too many colors can seem busy. Tiling your backsplash presents a great opportunity to introduce an accent color or a

■ *A tiled backsplash is the ideal place to add a decorative touch to your kitchen.*

striking pattern. You can use handmade or painted tiles, or create an eye-catching design that would be too distracting on a countertop.

Pattern

The classic tile pattern is a basic square grid; variations include diagonal grids, grids with small diamonds in the cut-off corners of larger tiles, herringbone patterns and brick-like overlapping layouts.

You can also use grout to affect the pattern. Grout of a contrasting color will create a bold look; a color that blends in with the tile will minimize the grid effect.

Size

Tile size is largely based on preference, but most people use 4-in. or 6-in. tile, given the small area. However, small tiles do mean more grout joints to clean and maintain.

Trim

Trim tiles are the pieces that finish off the edges of the countertop. These include bullnose tiles, with one or more rounded edges, L-shaped corner pieces, and V-cap pieces that finish the front of the countertop with an attractive, no-drip edge.

Solid-Surface Countertops

Solid surfacing has most of the attributes of the ideal countertop material: like stone, the color goes all the way through; like wood, it can be shaped and inlaid; like laminate, it comes in many colors; and like tile, it's durable and can be repaired. In fact, the only real drawback is its cost—typically $100 to $150 per linear foot installed. Although you can get granite and marble for almost the same price, natural stone counters lack the invisible seams of solid-surfacing, and blemishes can't be sanded out or refilled. So the real question with solid surfacing is how to get the best value for your investment.

Choosing a Style & Color

A good investment begins with color and style decisions. Most companies offer three or four design categories at different price levels. Solid colors cost the least; particles and mixed colors are more expensive. If the design you like best is out of your price range, don't give up and conclude that you can't afford solid surfacing. You can select a less costly color and use your first choice as an accent. In any case, do some comparison shopping; a similar pattern may be available for less from another company.

Solid-surface countertops are available in a range of finishes. As with other kitchen surfaces, matte or satin hides scratches better than a high sheen, and light colors tend to hide scratches better than dark colors. Fancy edges, large inlays (tile, granite or butcher block), and integral solid-surface sinks will all add to the cost. To save money, choose a stainless-steel sink and an edge that's easy to make (bevel or bullnose, for instance). If you do choose an integral solid-surface sink, be aware that sinks and countertops are often made from a different lot, which means the colors may not match exactly. You can avoid this problem by choosing a contrasting color for the sink or including an accent color stripe to separate the sink from the counter.

Working With a Fabricator

Since the top brands are similar in quality, the keys to a

■ *Top: Solid surfacing is ideal for custom shapes, such as the geometric corner details on this island.*

■ *Bottom: This curved countertop features a built-in drainboard that drains into an undermount sink.*

quality countertop are in its fabrication and installation. No matter who manufactures the solid-surfacing material you choose, a local fabricator will cut, shape and install it, so it's critical to find a good fabricator. Also, most manufacturers will honor their warranties only if the installation is done by a fabricator they've certified; do-it-yourself counters are rarely covered.

The fabricator will usually be chosen by your general contractor, cabinet dealer, kitchen designer or by a home center. If you hire a fabricator yourself, get three bids and check references, as usual. Although the fabrication time will be just a few days, the total lead time will be much more than that.

The fabricator will usually need to visit your home to take measurements after the base cabinets and the appliances next to the counters are in place. Here's what to look for in a quality installation.

• The counter should be leveled with shims, and the countertop should be supported by plywood strips, rather than a solid underlayment.

• All the seams should feel smooth, with no detectable dips or bumps. Since the seams joined on-site are weak points, they should be placed over a support strip. All seams should be at least 3 in. away from the sink and cooktop.

• Inside corners must be cut in perfect curves and sanded very smooth to withstand stress.

• The cooktop cutout should be protected by at least two layers of aluminum tape, which should be left hanging down under the counter (inside the cabinet) to dissipate heat.

• The finish should be consistent over the entire surface. To be sure, examine it from several points of view.

Making It Last

As tough as it is, a solid surface countertop does require some care. You can wipe up most stains and spills with soap and water. For stubborn stains, use a cleanser and a non-abrasive pad. On matte finishes, you can remove minor scratches by sanding with very fine

■ *The mirror-like surface of this sleek black countertop looks great but wouldn't be very practical for a family kitchen.*

sandpaper or a fine abrasive dish-scrubbing sponge, then buffing with a non-abrasive pad. High-gloss finishes require more buffing and, sometimes, polishing. Check with the manufacturer for specific care instructions.

Don't use a solid-surface countertop as a cutting board, as knives will scratch the surface. Also, don't place hot pots and pans directly on the counter.

If part of your counter is cut out for a sink, ask your fabricator for the waste piece. Save the piece as a source of perfectly color-matched patch material, in case your counter is ever damaged.

SOURCES
Solid-Surface Countertops

Avonite: 800/428-6648; www.avonite.com
DuPont (Corian): 800/426-7426; www.corian.com
Nevamar Corp (Fountainhead): 800/638-4380; www.nevamar.com
Ralph Wilson Plastics (Gibralter): 800/433-3222; www.wilsonart.com
Formica Corp (Surrell): 800/367-6422; www.formica.com
TRM Inc.: 800/766-2452; www.transolid.com

Sinks

The sink is where many of our kitchen chores are done—the only area used for both preparing meals and cleaning up after them. Although a good sink can last 15 years or more, eventually any sink will begin to show wear. If you're planning a kitchen remodel, it's always a good idea to replace both the sink and the faucet. Since you'll be living with them for a long time, shop carefully.

Fortunately, the kitchen sink is one of the most inexpensive components of a kitchen remodel. Although you can find high-end models with four-digit price tags, there are many well-made sinks starting at around $100. Here are some tips for buying a new sink and faucet.

Choosing a Material

The first step is to determine the kind of material that will suit your kitchen best—stainless steel, porcelain-on-cast-iron, solid surfacing, enamel-on-steel or composite materials. You can find durable, good-looking sinks in any of these materials; the question is which one best fits your lifestyle and the look of your new kitchen.

Stainless Steel

Stainless steel is attractive, easy to clean and readily available; it's also by far the most popular sink material. However, it does show water spots, and if the walls are too thin the sink will be noisy and dent easily. To avoid these problems, look for a sink made of at least 20-ga. steel (18-ga. is even better). For optimal corrosion resistance, make sure it has a high percentage of chromium and nickel; for example, a good stainless steel sink might contain 18 percent chromium and 8 percent nickel. These percentages should be in the product literature or on the manufacturer's Web site.

Stainless sinks were once notoriously noisy. However, even the less costly models now should have a factory-applied sound-deadening undercoating.

Also consider your finish options. For example, a brushed stainless finish is easier to clean than a glossy finish, and a steel-titanium alloy will give a sink a striking black cast.

Prices for a good-quality stainless sink start around $120 and range to over $1,000, but you can get a good double-bowl sink in the lower part of this range.

Porcelain-on-Cast-Iron

Porcelain-on-cast-iron sinks are durable, have a rich appearance and come in a wide range of designs and colors. To make sure you get a durable finish, buy a name brand, and look for a smooth, even surface. The sink should be free of chips and nicks, which can expose the bare iron and invite rust. Inspect the sink thoroughly before it's installed, especially around the rim, the drain and the bottom of the bowl.

For a tougher finish with the look of a cast-iron bowl, consider a fireclay sink—a vitreous-china product that has a strong, smooth finish and a very hard surface that doesn't show marks. Cast-iron and fireclay sinks both start around $200, but

■ *The brushed finish of these stainless-steel sink bowls is easier to clean than a glossy finish. The separate prep sink provides a convenient spot for washing vegetables when the main sink is stacked with dishes.*

■ *An integral solid-surface sink basin can be molded into almost any shape to fit your kitchen.*

can be considerably more than that, depending on a sink's size, color and features.

Solid Surfacing

If you select solid surfacing for your countertops, you can also install a sink of the same material (see **Solid-Surface Countertops**, pages 94-95). This approach offers a sleek, stylish look and a durable, easy-to-clean sink. Its biggest disadvantage is the cost; it can add as much as $700 to the price of your countertops. Also, don't expect to get a perfect color match with your countertops, since the sinks are often made from a different lot. A less expensive option is to purchase separately a solid surfacing sink that can be dropped into any countertop. Although this doesn't provide the same seamless look and rimless convenience as an integral sink, it can cost less than half as much.

Enamel-on-Steel

Enamel-on-steel is the least expensive sink material, starting at about $50. However, you get what you pay for, and in this case, that may mean an easily damaged finish and thin steel. A better-quality alternative is a steel sink with a porcelain finish and a polyester-resin backing. It will absorb shocks well and weigh half as much as a cast-iron sink. A typical double-bowl sink will run about $250.

TIP

Buying a New Faucet

When you buy a new sink, it's best to get a new faucet as well. As long as you spend at least $125 and get a name brand, you can be assured of a quality faucet. So the only things you really need to consider are the faucet's options, finishes and features, such as these:

OPTIONS

- A single handle faucet with a pull-out spout—stainless-steel hoses are best (starting around $325)
- A pot filler: a cold-water tap on a long arm near the cooktop (about $150, plus the new water line)
- A faucet with a water filter built into the spout (starting around $150)

FINISHES

- Chrome: still the most popular finish; it's durable and easy to clean
- Lifetime polished-brass finishes: warrantied not to tarnish, and they won't spot
- Satin-nickel finishes: warm and soft, they blend in with just about everything

FEATURES

- Washerless operation: This term covers ball, cartridge and ceramic-disk valve faucets. Ceramic-disk valves tend to last longest (especially if you have hard water), but all should last for years and are relatively easy to repair.
- A long spout: If your sink has three bowls, opt for a 12- to 14-in.-long spout.
- A spout that swivels at least 180 degrees: If you're buying a multiple bowl sink, you'll need that kind of flexibility to reach all the bowls.

Composite

Composite sinks, which are usually made of acrylics and quartz, are the newest entries in the sink market. Because the color goes all the way through, they hide nicks well. However, they haven't been widely accepted yet. Composite sinks start at about $250.

Determining Your Needs

Sink style options include single and multiple bowls in a wide range of sizes, shapes and depths. To narrow them down, consider the size of your kitchen and how you'll use the sink. For example, a large multiple basin sink would overpower a small kitchen. Instead, a standard 22×24-in. single-bowl model (which will have a bowl about 16×21 in.) would be a good choice for a kitchen that's less than 150 sq. ft. For a larger kitchen, you might consider a double or triple bowl that would allow you to stack dishes on one side while you rinse vegetables on the other.

For large kitchens, many designers now suggest including one main sink and a smaller bar sink. However, a second sink isn't usually necessary unless two or more cooks will be preparing meals at the same time. Even then, consider whether the plumbing upgrade and the $400 or so for the extra sink and faucet are worth it.

You'll also need to decide on these other sink considerations:

• Mounting style (see **Mounting Choices**, below): Self-rimming sinks are easiest to install; undermount sinks look sleek and make cleanup easy.

• Accessories: Sink add-ons include sprayers, soap and hand-lotion dispensers and filtered-water taps. The number of accessories you choose will determine how many holes you'll need in the sink deck.

• Color: You'll typically pay 15 to 40 percent more for a porcelain sink in any color other than white.

• Drain strainer: These are sold separately from the sink itself. They aren't expensive, but you do need to get the right kind for the style of your sink.

TIP

Mounting Choices

Plumbing a new sink is a fairly straightforward do-it-yourself job. However, you'll need to decide how you'll attach the sink to the countertop before you order the basin. There are basically three options.

A) Self-rimming sinks are the easiest to install—this job should only take you about an hour. Lighter sinks are secured to the counter with clips and screws, while heavy cast-iron sinks are held in place by their weight.

B) Some stainless-steel and enamel-on-steel sinks are held in place by a separate steel rim. The drawback of this approach is that you end up with two seams where dirt can accumulate.

C) Undermount sinks look sleek and make it easy to wipe stuff off the counters and into the sink. They also allow you to include sink bowls of different shapes and sizes. However, they take at least twice as long to install as self-rimming sinks. Also, since the edge of the counter will be exposed, it must be composed of a solid material, such as granite or solid surfacing.

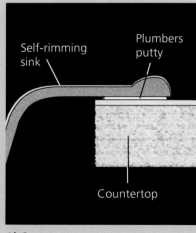

A) SELF-RIMMING

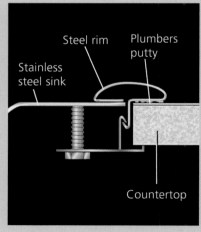

B) TOP MOUNT WITH RIM

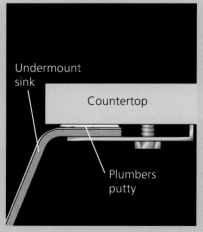

C) UNDERMOUNT

SOURCES

Sinks & Faucets

AMERICAN STANDARD: 800/223-0068;
www.americanstandard.com
BLANCO AMERICA: 856/829-2720;
www.blanco-america.com
CRANE PLUMBING: 800/347-6761; 800/877-6678;
www.craneplumbing.com
DELTA FAUCET: 800/345-3358; www.deltafaucet.com
ELJER PLUMBINGWARE: 800/423-5537; www.eljer.com
ELKAY: 630/572-3192; www.elkay.com
FRANKE: 800/626-5771; www.franke.com/ksd
GERBER PLUMBING FIXTURES: 847/675-6570;
www.gerberonline.com

GROHE: 630/582-7711; www.groheamerica.com
KALLISTA: 888/452-5547; www.kallistainc.com
KOHLER: 800/456-4537; www.kohlerco.com
KWC FAUCETS, INC.: 770/248-1600;
www.kwcfaucets.com
MOEN: 800/289-6636; www.moen.com
PEERLESS FAUCET: 800/438-6673;
www.peerless-faucet.com
PRICE PFISTER: 800/732-8238; www.PricePfister.com
STERLING PLUMBING: 888/783-7546;
www.sterlingplumbing.com

■ *Above: These under-mount sink bowls set in a solid–surface countertop provide a sleek look and make counter cleanup a breeze.*

■ *Right: A two–sink kitchen design allows two people to work together without getting in each other's way.*

APPLIANCES

Buying new appliances can be one of the most satisfying phases of a remodeling project, but it requires a fair amount of time and attention. Each type of appliance is available in an almost startling variety of types, styles and shapes; selecting the right models for your kitchen involves balancing the cost, performance, energy efficiency, convenience and style of each model you're considering. Since most appliances come in a few standard sizes, you may be able to plan your layout without knowing the exact brands or models you'll be installing. However, some appliances require structural modifications, so it's necessary to make some preliminary decisions early in the planning process.

The appliances in a typical U.S. home are responsible for about 20% of the household's energy consumption, according to the U.S. Department of Energy. Purchasing energy-wise appliances makes sense for your budget as well for the planet, and the essential information is easily accessible these days. Yellow *EnergyGuide* labels posted on all refrigerators, freezers, clothes washers and dishwashers sold in the U.S. provide an estimated annual operating cost and indicate the cost of operating the models with the highest and lowest annual operating cost. Comparison shopping for efficiency as well as features and price is greatly simplified by the wealth of information available on the internet. *Sources* throughout this section list web sites for major manufacturers; many buying guides and retail outlets have web sites as well.

■ *Opposite: By choosing quality appliances with time-saving conveniences that suit your lifestyle, you can make cooking and storing your food more pleasant and efficient.*
■ *Above: An island cooktop requires a good venting system, like this sleek vent hood.*

Ranges

Ranges, which are also known as stoves, combine an oven and a cooktop in one unit. Since a range often costs less and takes up less space than two separate units, it's a good option if your budget or space are limited.

The first step in buying a new range is deciding what best suits your kitchen and cooking style. The first and most obvious question is the source of power—gas, electricity or both. Traditionally, gas burners have been favored over electric coils because they allow for more immediate control of heat. Electric ovens, however, are known to cook more evenly than gas, and they tend to dry out the food less.

While these advantages and disadvantages still apply to most conventional ranges, technology is beginning to overcome the long-standing limitations of each power source. For example, new magnetic induction elements heat and cool almost immediately, and built-in heat deflectors resolve problems with uneven heat in gas ovens.

In most cases, though, selecting options is secondary; the most significant factor in your decision will be your current source of power. Although it's possible to convert to another power source—and remodeling offers that opportunity—after researching the options, you may not feel that the rewards justify the expense if you have to resort to a propane tank or run gas piping through the walls.

Standard dimensions for ranges are 30 in. and 36 in. wide; double-oven models can be much wider. Prices start at around $250 and go up to over $2,000. For more information about features for range ovens and cooktop burners, see **Cooktops** on page 106 and **Wall Ovens** on page 105; most of the available options offered for individual cooktops and wall ovens can also be found in range units.

Gas Ranges

Gas ranges use natural or liquid propane gas to fuel the cooktop burners and the oven. They also require a 120-volt, 20-amp outlet to power the oven light, timers and flame-ignition modules. Although the U.S. Department of Energy reports that only about 40% of American households currently cook with gas, it suggests that gas cooking is on the rebound. Among the reasons: electronic ignition reduces safety concerns surrounding pilot lights; gas ranges with electronic ignition cost less than half as much to operate as electric units; improved burner designs make newer models easier to clean than their predecessors.

Electric Ranges

Electric ranges use 240-volt current to heat the cooktop burners and the oven; they require a dedicated 50-amp electrical circuit. (Remember—if you're replacing a gas range with an electric model, you may need to have your electrical service upgraded.) Better electric ranges with such features as radiant-ribbon burners or microprocessors that regulate temperature utilize the natural advantages of electricity (safety, precise oven temperature control)

■ *A double-oven gas range tucked into a traditional brick alcove gives this kitchen plenty of cooking capacity, even for large gatherings.*

■ *The smooth ceramic surface of this range is attractive and easy to keep clean.*

while minimizing the disadvantages (burner response time, expense of operation).

Dual-fuel Ranges

Dual-fuel ranges combine the advantages of both gas and electric cooking: The cooktop surface uses gas, while the oven is electric. For some cooking enthusiasts, these ranges offer the best of both worlds in kitchens that don't have enough room for separate units.

Additional Options

All types of ranges come in a variety of configurations: freestanding, slide-in and drop-in. Freestanding ranges have finished side panels, so one or both sides can be exposed. Slide-in ranges are designed to fit into the space between two base cabinets, and so have unfinished sides. Drop-in ranges fit into special cabinets that are finished to match surrounding cabinets.

Double-oven Ranges

If you often find yourself juggling to bake one dish and broil another or to bake dishes at different temperatures and still have the whole meal ready at once, a double-oven range may be the perfect solution. You can expect a double-oven range to be more expensive than a comparable single-oven model, but the additional convenience can be well worth the investment.

Professional-style Ranges

A popular trend in kitchen appliances is professional-style ranges that have been modified for residential use. These ranges offer most of the cooking power and oven capacity of commercial units, but they are designed to be operated safely in a home kitchen.

If you select this type of range, make the decision during the early stages of your remodeling project—you'll need to plan ahead for the additional size and ventilation requirements.

Special Additions

Consider ranges that offer extras, such as a modular cooktop that allows you to easily substitute a grill or griddle plate for a set of burners. Depending on the layout of the kitchen, you may also need to purchase a unit with a built-in downdraft vent. And if you entertain frequently or your mealtimes are often staggered, you may find a warming drawer particularly useful. This unit, which replaces the storage drawer at the bottom of the range, keeps prepared food warm for up to two hours.

SOURCES

Ranges

AMANA: 800/843-0304; www.amana.com
FRIGIDAIRE: 800/288-4924; www.frigidaire.com
GE APPLIANCES: 800/626-2000; www.geappliances.com
JENN-AIR: 800/536-6247; www.jennair.com
KITCHENAID: 800/422-1230; www.kitchenaid.com
MAGIC CHEF: 800/688-9900; www.maytagcorp.com
MAYTAG: 800/688-9900; www.maytag.com
ROPER: 800/447-6737; www.roperappliances.com
SEARS (KENMORE): 800/349-4358; www.sears.com
VIKING RANGE: 601/451-4133; www.vikingrange.com
WHITE-WESTINGHOUSE: 800/288-4924
WHIRLPOOL: 800/253-1301; www.whirlpool.com
WOLF: 310-637-3737; www.wolfrange.com

Microwave Ovens

It isn't hard to see why the microwave oven is now the most popular cooking appliance for many families. A microwave is much quicker and more efficient than a standard oven and doesn't heat up the kitchen in summer. It's the ideal way to defrost frozen foods, heat beverages and leftovers and prepare frozen dinners.

Despite their popularity, microwaves do have some drawbacks. For example, they don't brown meats and baked goods like conventional ovens. And since you can't use metal in most microwaves, you'll probably need to invest in a set of microwave-safe glass, ceramic or plastic cooking and storage containers. Microwaves also tend to cook unevenly, although most manufacturers address this issue with heat-distribution systems or turntables.

If you don't have a microwave yet, consider adding one during your remodeling project. Some households even include two of them—one by the cooktop to melt butter and defrost frozen foods and another by the refrigerator to prepare snacks and leftovers.

Shopping Tips

Since most microwave ovens are priced in a relatively narrow range, between $100 and $400, your selection should be based on how many features you want, how much space you have and how much microwave cooking you plan to do. Cooking power—measured in watts—is another consideration. Seven hundred to 800 watts is ample power for a small microwave, while mid-size and large models should have at least 1000 watts.

There are three types of microwave ovens: basic, sensor and convection. If you'll mostly be reheating meals, defrosting food or popping corn, get a basic microwave. Most have automatic settings that set the time and power level for various foods. The next step up is a sensor microwave that has more sophisticated automatic controls. For example, some of them will measure the moisture of the food and automatically shut off the power when it's done, to avoid overcooking. Finally, you can get a convection microwave that combines the functions of a microwave and a convection oven in one unit. These models allow you to switch over to conventional heat to bake pies and charbroil roasts.

Microwaves come in many sizes, from ½-cu.-ft. models that rest on a countertop or hang beneath a cupboard to 1½-cu.-ft. built-in units. If you're not sure where to put your new microwave, try to place it near your food preparation area, and be sure to allow at least 1½ in. on all sides for ventilation. Also, don't connect your microwave to the same electrical circuit as your refrigerator or other high-amp appliance; if the microwave's power output is reduced, foods may not cook properly.

To size your microwave, measure the space you have in mind, allowing enough room to open the door fully. To make sure the cooking area will be large enough, bring a plate or cooking dish along with you to the store.

If you're tight on counter space, consider an over-the-range unit that includes an integral venting system and task lighting for the cooktop. Be aware that this placement can be hazardous for children and may limit your space for working at the range.

■ *This cooking center includes a space-saving microwave installed over a range of the same style. The microwave has a 300 cfm integral vent fan and task lighting for the cooktop.*

Wall Ovens

Some kitchen layouts call for—and some cooks prefer—wall ovens. Manufacturers offer single- and double-oven units, and again, your choices include gas and electric.

Although the oven types discussed here represent widely available options, appliance manufacturers continue to search for faster, more efficient ways to produce superior results. For example, light ovens have entered the market and may become widely used in the near future. Using infrared and visible light, these units produce grill-quality food at incredibly fast rates—as little as two minutes for a roast pork loin.

A note about a self-cleaning feature, some form of which is available on most electric wall ovens and ranges. The higher insulation levels on self-cleaning ovens reduces their energy consumption for normal cooking. However, be aware that if you use the self-cleaning option more than once a month, you offset any potential savings in energy costs.

■ *This wall oven has a coordinated warming drawer that keeps foods hot until you're ready to serve them.*

Conventional Ovens

Conventional ovens (also called radiant or thermal heat ovens) use two heating elements: one on the bottom for baking and roasting, and another on top for broiling. To reduce the problem of uneven heating, new ovens are designed so that the bottom heating element shuts off periodically during the standard bake cycle, allowing for more even cooking.

Convection Ovens

Convection ovens feature a fan that blows hot air around the oven, maintaining even temperatures and reducing cooking times by at least 25%. The increased air circulation makes convection ovens fantastic for baking—you can even bake cookies on every shelf at once. However, they can be somewhat noisy.

Many ovens with the convection feature allow you to switch between convection and conventional modes.

SOURCES

Microwave & Wall Ovens

AMANA: 800/843-0304; www.amana.com
FRIGIDAIRE: 800/288-4924; www.frigidaire.com
GE APPLIANCES: 800/626-2000; www.geappliances.com
JENN-AIR: 800/536-6247; www.jennair.com
KITCHENAID: 800/422-1230; www.kitchenaid.com
MAYTAG: 800/688-9900; www.maytag.com
PANASONIC: 800/211-7262; www.panasonic.com
ROPER: 800/447-6737; www.roperappliances.com
SAMSUNG: www.samsung.com
SEARS (KENMORE): 800/349-4358; www.sears.com
SHARP ELECTRONICS: 800/237-4277; www.sharp-usa.com
VIKING RANGE: 601/451-4133; www.vikingrange.com
WHIRLPOOL: 800/253-1301; www.whirlpool.com

■ *One of the advantages of placing a cooktop on an island is that you can surround it with plenty of countertop working space.*

Cooktops

A cooktop is essentially the heating element of a range packaged in a unit that fits into an opening in a countertop. Here again, you have a choice between gas and electricity, and there are advantages to each.

When comparing power sources, it helps to know that gas burners are measured in Btus (British thermal units); electric burners in watts. The higher the rating, the more powerful the burner. For the sake of comparison, you can estimate that a 2,400w coil burner delivers approximately the cooking power of a 15,000 Btu gas burner.

Standard dimensions for cooktops range from 30 to 48 in. wide, and prices vary widely. Basic electric coil models start at around $200; gas models at about $300. Glass cooktops will run you closer to $500, and the upper range for any type can easily reach $1,000.

Electric

Traditional resistance coil cooktops are slow to heat, cool and respond to adjustments. Still, they're less expensive than other types of cooktops and have many fans. For one thing, tests recently conducted by *Consumer Reports* showed that when compared to gas burners of comparable ratings "a coil burner...still holds the (speed) record for bringing a large pot of water to a near boil."

Ceramic glass cooktops (often called *smooth-tops*) have a smooth ceramic-glass panel that covers the entire cooking surface. These sleek and easy-to-clean units can be found in nearly 25% of the homes in North America. Burner options include radiant-ribbon, halogen and magnetic induction.

Radiant-ribbon burners are similar to resistance coils but have a greater surface area, which means they heat up and cool down much more quickly than traditional coils. This is the most common type of smoothtop burner.

Halogen burners use a halogen gas bulb for heat. They offer precise control, rapid heating and even cooking, but they're more expensive than radiant-ribbon burners and aren't available in as many models.

Magnetic induction elements convey heat from an induction coil directly to the pan. Response to adjustment is almost immediate and cooking times are reduced by up to 20%. Induction burners require that you use cast iron or steel cookware.

Another nice cooktop feature is electronic controls, which replace traditional knob or dial controls. Because these respond to fingertip pressure, they can be easier to operate for people with manual difficulties. They're also easier to clean because the control panel is a flush surface.

Gas

Gas cooktops are fueled by natural or liquid propane gas and are available with open or sealed burners. Open burners have an opening around the burner through which spills fall onto a cleanup tray below. Some open burners have metal rings that help catch spills. With sealed burners, a continuous metal tray encloses everything except the burner head. Spills are contained on the cooktop surface, making cleanup easy.

A good gas burner (or set of burners) should provide very high and low heat: 15,000 Btus is about the high mark for professional-style burners; 500 Btus is great for a gentle simmer. If you're planning to run a cooktop on propane rather than natural gas, make sure that conversion is possible, and ask whether it will result in any loss of power.

SOURCES

Cooktops

ALL SOURCES LISTED ON PAGE 103 OFFER COOKTOPS.

Vent Fans

Vent fans protect your kitchen surfaces and your health by exhausting the heat, steam, grease and odors produced by cooking. Since your local codes may have specific requirements, check with a building inspector or HVAC contractor before you choose a venting system.

Vent fans are rated for air flow (in cubic feet per minute, or cfm) and noise level (in sone). Look for a unit with a high air-flow rating and a noise rating of 1 sone or less—about as loud as a refrigerator (although more powerful units tend to be louder).

There are two main types of vent fan systems: hoods installed over a range or cooktop and down-draft units built into the cooktop or installed behind it.

Range & Vent Hoods

Range and vent hoods sit over a cooktop or range, typically mounted under wall cabinets, and come in ducted and ductless versions. A ducted hood filters the air and vents it to the outdoors, while a ductless unit simply recirculates the air through a filter. While ductless hoods may seem like a bargain, they're far less effective (and prohibited in some areas) and should be avoided; they provide neither adequate ventilation nor filtering. Vent hoods—typically used over an island cooktop—extend down from the ceiling and are ducted to the outside.

Over a range, a hood should extend 3 in. on either side. You'll need 120 cfm for light cooking on a standard range and 200 to 400 cfm for heavy cooking. Over an island, the hood should be the same size as the cooktop, with a minimum of 180 cfm; 450 to 600 is better. A professional-style cooktop or range needs additional power: 1 cfm for every 100 Btus delivered by all burners.

With conventional appliances, install the vent or range hood 24 to 30 in. above the cooking surface; with professional-style units, install it 30 to 36 in. above.

Basic wall-mounted hoods start at around $50, but $200 to $500 gets you more features and power. Custom hoods can run from $800 to more than $2,000.

■ *Specialized grills and wok burners with a high heat output require a heavy-duty ducted ventilation system.*

Down-Draft Systems

Down-draft systems have a built-in fan that pulls air from the cooktop down and into a ducting system. They're popular for modular ranges and cooktops, especially on islands. Down-draft vents must be more powerful than standard vents, because they work against the natural upward flow of heated air. They are less effective for tall stockpots and burners that are farther from the vent. A down-draft vent should provide 300-500 cfm, depending on the cooktop size and your cooking habits. Cooktops with down-draft fans start at around $600; retrofitting an existing cooktop with a down-draft system can cost $600 or more.

Ducting it Right

A vent's performance is affected by its ductwork; keep it short and straight: 30 ft. or less is best. Also minimize turns and size transitions, and vent the ductwork outside, not to the attic or basement.

SOURCES

Vent Fans

Broan-Nutone: 800/548-0790; www.broan-nutone.com
Faber: 508/358-5353; www.faberonline.com
Rangecraft: 800/337-2643; www.rangecraft.com
Venmar: 800/567-3855; www.venmar-ventilation.com
Vent-A-Hood: 214/235-5201
Viking Range: 601/451-4133; www.vikingrange.com

Refrigerators

As you're deciding whether or not to purchase a new refrigerator for your newly remodeled kitchen, there's more to consider than appearance. Even if your current unit fits in the new space and matches the color scheme, it may make sense to replace it. Newer models offer greater convenience; they also offer much better energy efficiency, and that translates to dollars and cents.

Refrigerators use more energy than any other kitchen appliance—as much as a sixth of all electricity used in American homes. Advances in technology have cut the energy consumption of refrigerators by about 60% over the last twenty years. Annual operating costs for standard refrigerators range between $71 and $129. As with other appliances, compare the ratings on the yellow *EnergyGuide* labels on the units you are considering.

Refrigerators are widely available in two styles: slide-in and built-in.

• *Slide-in refrigerators* are the traditional choice. They're available in many sizes and configurations, typically

SOURCES

Refrigerators

AMANA: 800/843-0304; www.amana.com
FRIGIDAIRE: 800/288-4924; www.frigidaire.com
GE APPLIANCES: 800/626-2000; www.geappliances.com
JENN-AIR: 800/536-6247; www.jennair.com
KITCHENAID: 800/422-1230; www.kitchenaid.com
MAYTAG: 800/688-9900; www.maytag.com
MIELE: 800/843-7231; www.mieleusa.com
ROPER: 800/447-6737; www.roperappliances.com
SEARS (KENMORE): 800/349-4358; www.sears.com
SUB-ZERO FREEZER: 608/271-2233; www.subzero.com
TRAULSEN & CO.: 800/825-8220; www.traulsen.com
WHIRLPOOL: 800/253-1301; www.whirlpool.com
WHITE-WESTINGHOUSE: 800/288-4924

ranging from 28 to 34 in. deep. There are also 24-in. deep models, to which you can add panels that match your cabinets. This option lets you achieve a built-in look at a lower price.

• *Built-in refrigerators* are wider than most slide-ins but are only 24 in. deep, so they end up flush with the front of your base cabinets. Most have a side-by-side freezer configuration. The front and sides can be finished to match your kitchen cabinets or other surfaces. Some built-ins have non-standard dimensions; be sure to check the exact size of the model you're considering.

When planning the position of your refrigerator in a new kitchen layout, leave enough room to open the door all the way. If you're adding a built-in refrigerator, you'll also need to leave room for venting above the unit. Remember, too, that refrigerators need a dedicated electrical circuit.

Freezer Configurations

Most refrigerators have one of three kinds of freezer configurations; compact refrigerators and under-the-counter refrigeration drawers are also available.

• *Top freezer* units are probably the most common refrigerator configuration. They have a

■ *The stainless-steel panels on this built-in side-by-side refrigerator/ freezer fit in beautifully with the clean lines of the kitchen.*

solution where space is at a premium, such as dorm rooms or studio apartments.

• *Under-the-counter* units are either small standing units or drawer-style refrigerators or freezers that allow you to keep produce or other chilled items conveniently close to your dining or food preparation area. However, they can be quite costly compared to other types.

Refrigerator Features

When buying a refrigerator, look for quality construction, quiet operation and convenient features. Balance the cost of each option with its impact on the efficiency of your kitchen. Some features that many homeowners find essential include door bins that hold gallon milk jugs, adjustable pullout shelves and separate temperature and humidity controls for meat, fruit and vegetable compartments.

You may also want to consider options such as:

• An automatic icemaker. This convenience adds $75 to $250 to the price and 14 to 20% to the energy consumption of a refrigerator.

• A built-in water filter for drinking water.

• A refreshment center that allows you to access snacks and beverages without opening the door of the main compartment, which adds to the cost but also to the convenience and may reduce energy consumption.

• Microprocessor temperature and humidity controls.

■ *Above: The refreshment center in this side-by-side refrigerator is an energy-saving feature that allows you to access snacks and beverages without opening the main door.*

■ *Lower right: These refrigerated drawers keep fresh produce conveniently close to the food preparation counter—another option when planning your work triangle.*

freezer over the refrigerator, with a total storage capacity that can range from 14 to 25 cubic feet, depending on the model. Some of them also feature in-door ice and water dispensers. Top freezers also use 7-13% less energy than side-by-side models in a similar size.

• *Side-by-side freezer* units have a vertical freezer compartment next to the refrigerator compartment, and a total capacity from 19 to 30 cubic feet. Many side-by-side units have in-door water and ice dispensers. Although they offer an elegant look, they're more expensive to purchase and to operate than the other configurations.

• *Bottom freezer* units place the freezer below the refrigerator, which moves the refrigerator shelves to a more convenient position, but makes the freezer harder to access. They typically have a capacity of 15 to 22 cubic feet. A bottom freezer unit wastes less energy when the freezer door is opened and closed frequently. These units don't offer in-door ice and water dispensers.

• *Compact* refrigerators range from 1.5 to 7 cubic feet in capacity. They're the ideal

Dishwashers

The dishwasher is an essential part of a modern American kitchen, and there are good reasons to consider investing in a new one even if your old unit is still working fine. A newer dishwasher will hold more dishes, use less water and energy and work more quietly and effectively—all without breaking your budget.

The 24-in. standard depth of most dishwashers places them flush with standard base cabinets. However, you can also find non-standard dimensions and freestanding units. The freestanding units offer the most flexibility; they can be hidden in a closet and rolled out on casters to attach to the sink. Most can also be converted to serve as a built-in unit.

Most dishwashers run between $300 and $500—but at any price level, the key issues to consider in buying a dishwasher are operating costs, noise reduction, cleaning power and features.

Operating Costs

To find out how much a dishwasher costs to run, check its yellow *EnergyGuide* tag. By law, American-made dishwashers must use less than 2.17 kilowatt-hours of electricity per wash cycle and must have a low-energy air-dry option. The operating cost is also affected by your water heater. It's roughly 45% cheaper to run a dishwasher when it's fed by a gas water heater rather than an electric one. Energy prices fluctuate, but today's dishwashers will cost you around $17 to $34 a year to run.

Also check how much water the unit requires; new models typically use 6.5 to 9 gal. of water per cycle, and some European models use as little as 5 gal. per cycle. Bear in mind that a dishwasher that doesn't require you to rinse the dishes before loading saves water.

Reducing Noise

Although dishwashers have traditionally been the noisiest of the major appliances, they're now quieter than ever before. The racket is caused by motor vibration and water splashing against the door. Manufacturers have reduced noise by modifying the motor and improving sound-absorbing insulation. Lower-price machines typically have insulation behind the door and over the sides of the housing. Medium-price machines usually have additional insulation on top. Premium models may be double-insulated with insulation over the tub, behind the door, over the top, sides and back, inside the doors and behind the access panel and toekick. To find out how noisy a unit is, ask to hear the showroom model in operation.

Cleaning Power

A dishwasher's cleaning power depends on how it disperses and filters water. Spinning spray arms disperse water and towers shoot water up from the center. Most machines have two or three "wash levels"—arrays of spray arms and towers. A two-level system might have a bottom spray for dishes in the lower rack and another for dishes in the upper rack. Since it's the direct spray of water that loosens dried food, the more dishes the spray reaches, the better. Two or three levels is plenty for most households, and how the water is aimed is more important than the number of spray arms and towers.

■ *If you raise your dishwasher to make it easier to use, be sure to use a base that can support the weight of the appliance while it's operating.*

SOURCES

Dishwashers

AMANA: 800/843-0304; www.amana.com
ASKO: 972/238-0794; www.asko.com
FRIGIDAIRE: 800/288-4924; www.frigidaire.com
GE APPLIANCES: 800/626-2000; www.geappliances.com
JENN-AIR: 800/536-6247; www.jennair.com
KITCHENAID: 800/422-1230; www.kitchenaid.com
MAGIC CHEF: 800/688-9900; www.maytagcorp.com
MAYTAG: 800/688-9900; www.maytag.com
MIELE: 800/843-7231; www.mieleusa.com
ROPER: 800/447-6737; www.roperappliances.com
SEARS (KENMORE): 800/349-4358; www.sears.com
WHIRLPOOL: 800/253-1301; www.whirlpool.com
WHITE-WESTINGHOUSE: 800/288-4924

■ *The sleek design of this dishwasher includes touchpad controls and a concealed door handle.*

All dishwashers have a filter to keep the wash water free of food particles, and many units have two. Some also have a grinder blade that slices up particles and unclogs filters.

Setting Options

Most dishwashers have three settings: a light cycle, a normal cycle and a heavy, or pot, cycle. However, some machines offer other specialized cycles, such as these:

Rinse-and-Hold

This is helpful if your family takes a few days to fill the dishwasher. It allows you to rinse the dishes without washing them, to prevent dried-on food particles.

China and Crystal

This cycle reduces the heat, cycle time and spray intensity to protect fine china and crystal. However, unless you entertain a lot and do no handwashing, the added expense probably isn't worth it.

Delay-Start

This feature allows you to run a cycle after you've gone to bed, when the power rates are lowest. Set-ahead times vary from 4 to 14 hours.

High-Temperature

This features raises the dishwasher's water temperature from the normal setting (120° to 140°F) to about 160°F. The extra heat helps loosen dried-on food particles and sanitize dishes. However, it consumes much more energy and can fog windows.

TIP

What to Look For in a Dishwasher

SPRAY ARMS
- More spray arms & towers to aim water effectively
- More spray jets to spray water in more directions

RACKS
- Removable and height-adjustable upper racks to allow tall items below
- Terraced bottoms to allow oversize items below
- Stemware holders
- Fold-down tines to accommodate large items
- Fold-down shelves to allow double-stacking

SILVERWARE BASKETS
- Lidded compartments for small items
- Utensil basket in a recessed door compartment to maximize space in lower rack

SOUND REDUCTION
- Fiberglass insulation
- An underlayer of Mylar, asphalt or rubber material
- Insulating materials in or behind the door
- Motor modifications

FILTRATION SYSTEM
- Food-grinder blades and dual filters to break down and remove food particles

WALLS, CEILINGS & FLOORS

The walls, ceilings and floors of your new kitchen will form the backdrop for all the other elements you've selected so carefully. Since you use the kitchen every day, it's important to provide a soothing background with lasting appeal. Because of this, a simple wall and ceiling treatment works best in most kitchens.

Kitchen walls are typically painted or covered with wallpaper, and the ceilings are usually finished in a light color that reflects light and makes the room appear brighter. For a more dramatic effect, you can cover walls with solid surfacing, ceramic tile, wood or metal panels or mirrors. As a general rule, all kitchen surfaces should be smooth and washable. Avoid porous or deeply textured materials, such as spray texture, acoustic tiles, unfinished wood or suspended ceiling panels, as smoke and grease will collect on these surfaces and ruin them.

Because of the time you'll spend standing on it and the significant visual impact it will have on your new kitchen, it's important that the floor is both comfortable and attractive. You can also use flooring to highlight specific areas or to help solve layout problems (see **Designing with Flooring**, pages 120-121).

Any new flooring you choose will need a smooth, solid subfloor, and it's difficult to determine the condition of the existing subfloor before the old flooring is removed. For this reason, it's wise to build one or two flex days into your schedule to prepare the subfloor for finished flooring. In some cases, you'll need to add a layer: cementitious backer board for ceramic tile and underlayment for vinyl flooring. If you plan to install the flooring yourself, call in a professional to assess the condition of the subfloor before you continue.

■ *Opposite: This beautiful kitchen features a white ceiling, a wood floor that matches the cabinetry and sliding walls that can hide the kitchen from view.* ■ *Above: The cozy look of this kitchen is due to a combination of deep forest green paint, richly stained woodwork and plentiful natural and artificial light.*

Paint

A simple paint or wallcovering treatment is one of the most effective ways to unify all the different design elements in the typical kitchen, especially if the kitchen is small or the amount of visible wall space is limited.

Kitchen walls and ceilings require a protective finish that's durable, water-resistant and easy to clean. The most common finish is gloss enamel paint—it's inexpensive, easy to apply and meets all the above requirements.

If you're replacing the flooring or cabinets in your kitchen, complete the painting before the new things are installed; you won't have to be as careful with the paint, and even if the installers make a few marks on the wall, you can easily touch up the wall after they're done.

Coordinating Colors

When selecting paint for kitchen walls, choose colors that will complement, rather than compete with, your cabinets, countertops and flooring. It's easiest to do this if you bring along samples of these materials while shopping for the paint. A large decorating center or paint store can offer more than a thousand colors to choose from, and by comparing your samples with the store's paint swatches, you'll be able to narrow down the options far more quickly.

Here are a few tips for selecting paint colors for your kitchen.

• Light colors make a room seem bigger.

• Dark colors make a room seem smaller.

• Cool colors (blue tones) recede from the eye, creating a calm or peaceful effect.

■ *This kitchen boasts simply painted walls, a color-washed alcove and rough-cut ceiling beams stained with a light pigment that reveals the grain.*

• Warm colors (red tones) advance toward the eye, creating a more lively or dramatic effect.

• Dark colors are good for hiding unevenness in walls and other surface flaws.

• Pale colors are usually the best choice for rooms that will be used every day, such as the kitchen.

If you don't trust your ability to pick colors that will complement your kitchen, you can seek the help of a kitchen designer or interior decorator, or look for ideas in design books, home magazines or kitchen showrooms. Also, many decorating centers have design consultants who will assist you at no additional charge.

Selecting Paint

Don't make a final decision about paint color based on the store's sample chips; they're often not an accurate representation of the final color. Instead, buy a quart of the color you have in mind and paint a sample area on the wall or on a piece of white cardboard or drywall.

Over the next day or two, place your painted sample

next to the other sample materials for your new kitchen and examine it from different angles and in different lighting conditions. You'll notice that the appearance of the color changes dramatically as the light changes.

Paint finishes range from flat (matte) formulations to high-gloss enamels. Enamel paints in gloss and semi-gloss dry to a shiny finish; they're the best choice for woodwork and surfaces that need to withstand moisture and frequent cleaning, as is the case with most kitchen walls. For less gloss, ask for an "egg shell" finish or formulations specially designed for kitchen walls.

You'll also need to decide between water-based (latex) and alkyd-based (oil) paint. Latex paint is now the most common choice, especially among do-it-yourself painters. Unlike alkyd paint, latex paint is low-odor, easy to use and clean up, and suitable for almost every application. Although today's latex formulations are designed to go right over most alkyd paints, the one exception is old gloss finishes, which you'll need to sand lightly before repainting. In a kitchen, most of the old paint you'll find will have a gloss finish.

When it comes to paint quality, don't skimp. The cost of the paint is small compared to the cost of the labor involved (or your own time and effort). Buy the best paint you can afford, and you'll see a big difference in coverage, wear and washability—which will mean less work for you, both during painting and over the long run.

Preparing to Paint

Painting is one remodeling job that many homeowners decide to tackle themselves. However, resist the impulse to just crack open a can of paint and start rolling it onto the walls. Paint adheres best to a clean, sound surface, and a high-gloss finish will highlight any imperfections in the walls or ceiling. The key to a long-lasting, good-looking paint job is preparing the surface properly.

Start by cleaning the surface thoroughly. You can use trisodium phosphate (TSP) on greasy walls, and bleach on mildewed areas. Next, scrape off any old paint or residue and sand all the rough spots smooth. If the old paint is gloss, sand the entire surface lightly with 120-grit sandpaper, so that the new paint will adhere to it.

■ *To unify the many visual elements of this kitchen, all the cabinetry and woodwork was painted a warm eggshell, and a few accent colors were added to provide variety.*

Fill in any holes, cracks or gouges with spackling compound. Apply a white shellac to stains, to prevent them from bleeding through the new topcoat. Finally, you'll need to apply a primer, especially if you're painting over new drywall, bare wood, masonry or any other porous surface.

SOURCES
Paint

ACE HARDWARE (PAINT): 630/990-6522; www.acehardware.com
BEHR (HOME DEPOT): 770/433-8211; www.homedepot.com
BENJAMIN MOORE & CO.: 800/826-2623; www.benjaminmoore.com
DULUX & GLIDDEN: 800/984-5444; www.duluxpaint.com
DUTCH BOY: 800/828-5669
KRYLON: 800/457-9566
PRATT & LAMBERT: 800/289-7728
SEARS: 800/972-4687; www.sears.com
SHERWIN-WILLIAMS: 800/474-3794; www.sherwin.com
VALSPAR CORP.: 800/345-4530; www.valspar.com
WM. ZINSSER & CO.: 732/469-4367; www.zinsser.com

Wallpaper

Very few "wallpapers" are actually made exclusively of paper anymore. Instead, they may be composed of textiles, vinyl, vinyl-coated paper or cloth, natural grasses, foil or Mylar®. However, on kitchen walls it's best to avoid textured wallpaper and stick with vinyl or vinyl-coated wallcoverings. They're easy to install and maintain, and they hold up better than other coverings in a kitchen setting. For best results, get a *scrubbable* paper—one designed to withstand regular scrubbing, or a *washable* paper, which will tolerate occasional sponging.

Wallcoverings come with various kinds of backings and removal options. *Prepasted* papers are backed with an adhesive and don't require any additional paste. *Peelable* papers can be pulled off the wall, leaving behind a paper backing that acts as a liner for a new wallcovering. (If you decide to paint the wall, you'll have to scrape it off.) *Strippable* papers leave little residue when they're removed.

■ *This striped wallpaper echoes the red countertop and provides a bold contrast with the white cabinetry and windows.*

Choosing Pattern & Texture

Wallpaper offers you the opportunity to choose from a wide range of patterns and textures. Since kitchen walls are generally best kept simple, choose a wallcovering that will blend in rather than stand out, especially for a small kitchen. However, in many kitchens an all-over wallpaper pattern or texture can be very effective—you can even use it to fool the eye into thinking that the room is larger or smaller. Here are a few tips for using wallpaper patterns and textures.

• A small print can make a small space seem bigger.
• A large pattern can make a large space seem more intimate.
• A horizontal pattern will expand a short room.
• A vertical pattern will emphasize a room's height.
• A geometric motif can make a shallow room appear deeper.
• A smooth surface will reflect more light, making the room appear slightly brighter.
• A textured surface will hold more shadow, making the room appear slightly darker.
• A subtle pattern may become less prominent or even become unnoticeable once it's installed next to more

related borders or accent designs; these elements can be an easy and inexpensive way to give your kitchen a custom-designed look.

When selecting borders and accents, bear in mind how they'll affect the perceived shape of your kitchen. For example, a dark border along the top of the walls can make a ceiling look lower. This might be cozy in a roomy, well-lighted kitchen with a high ceiling, but it could make a small kitchen feel even more closed-in.

prominent design elements.

• A delicate, airy pattern (such as scattered sprays of flowers) can make a small room feel more expansive.

• A dense, curvy pattern (such as large roses) can make a large room feel more intimate.

Decorators suggest that a well-designed room should have a satisfying balance of colors, patterns and textures. However, in most kitchens the flooring, appliances and counters all tend to have cool, smooth surfaces, which means that wallcovering is one of the few areas where you can choose from a range of visual-texture effects. If you're seeking a clean, streamlined look, a smooth or glossy wallpaper will enhance this effect even further. If you're looking to soften the mood of the room, select a matte wallcovering, perhaps with a subtle pattern.

When choosing a wallpaper pattern, always get a large sample and view it from a distance as well as close up. To get an idea of how it will work on a large scale, squint your eyes and look away, then look back at the pattern. This will help you discern the lines and shapes that make up the underlying structure of the pattern, as well as its tonal values.

Using Borders & Accents

Interior designers say that patterns are most effective when you combine different scales or weights of one theme in the room. To help you do this, many wallpaper patterns are now grouped into design families that allow you to select from a variety of coordinated patterns, borders and design accents, including frescoes, watercolors, stain-like finishes and other classic schemes. Check to see if the wallcovering patterns you like best have any

Doing it Yourself

Although many homeowners tackle the job themselves, putting up wallpaper can be more complicated and difficult than it appears. If you've never done it before, you should probably hire a professional, especially if your pattern requires careful matching or your walls are divided into a lot of small spaces that will require careful cutting. Even if you have some experience, consider the complexity of the pattern, the layout of your walls and your level of expertise before you decide to do it yourself. If your skills need some brushing up or you want to review the basics, consult a good book on wallpapering before you begin.

SOURCES

Wallpaper

AMERICAN BLIND & WALLPAPER FACTORY: 800/735-5300, www.abwf.com

ARCHETONIC: 914/969-4363

DULUX: 800/984-5444; www.duluxpaint.com

EISENHART: 800/931-9255

F. SCHUMACHER & CO. (GRAMERCY): 800/332-3384; www.fschumacher.com

INTERNATIONAL WALLCOVERINGS: 905/791-1547

LAURA ASHLEY: 800/367-2000; www.lauraashley.com

SHERWIN-WILLIAMS: 800/474-3794; www.sherwin.com

SUNWORTHY WALLCOVERINGS: 800/791-8594; www.sunworthy.com

THIBAULT WALLCOVERINGS: 800/223-0704

WM. ZINSSER & CO.: 732/469-4367; www.zinsser.com

Beyond Paint & Wallpaper

Most kitchen walls and ceilings begin and end with paint and wallpaper—but if you'd like to be a bit more adventurous, there are other options. Some of the ideas that follow are better suited for roomy kitchens with good lighting and a simple design scheme; they involve using textured materials that tend to crowd a small space. Also, keep in mind that some of these options aren't as easy to keep clean as gloss paint or vinyl wallpaper.

Ceramic Tile, Stone & Brick

Tile, stone and brick can be effective ways to cover an alcove or backsplash or to cover the lower half of an open wall. If you're tiling a backsplash, consider investing in top-quality hand-painted tiles. Since this is usually a small area, it won't cost that much, and it can be the finishing touch that turns your kitchen into a showplace. For more information, including a list of sources, see **Ceramic Tile Countertops,** pages 92-93.

If you decide to install ceramic wall tiles yourself, make sure you take time to learn the proper installation techniques. For example, ceramic tile contractors use a cementitious backer board or a thick mortar base as backing for wall tile.

Wood Paneling

Wood paneling can add charm and character to your kitchen—just make sure the room has enough good lighting to counteract the warming effect of the wood. Also, be sure to protect any bare wood surfaces from grease, smoke and moisture by sealing them with protective layers of polyurethane varnish or gloss paint.

Sheet paneling is typically made of hardboard or plywood and is installed with panel adhesive and nails. Panels that are milled with vertical grooves offer a traditional look. For a more contemporary style, choose a quality plywood with hardwood veneer, then finish it with a clear polyurethane varnish.

Another option is softwood plank paneling (typically pine, fir, cedar or redwood), which is installed one board at a time rather than in sheets. It's available in many styles, thicknesses and patterns, and can be used horizontally, vertically or diagonally. Most planks come with tongue-and-groove or shiplap edges. Better-quality plank paneling usually has to be special-ordered from a lumberyard or home center.

Molding

Moldings are used to dress up window and door openings, cover transitions between floors, walls and ceilings, or to add a decorative touch to a plain wall. Wood moldings are commonly available in pine and oak in just about any style you can think of. Like paneling, unfinished wood moldings must be protected by paint or polyurethane varnish.

If you plan to paint the woodwork, choose *finger jointed* molding. This "paint grade" molding is less expensive than other types because each piece is made up of several smaller pieces joined together. Some paint grade products are available pre-primed. If you're using a clear finish or a stain on your molding, look for "clear" molding that's milled from a single piece of wood. Also make sure the coloring and grain patterns of the different molding pieces are similar.

■ *This kitchen features a paneled ceiling with exposed joists, a tile backsplash and a brick alcove.*

Popular alternatives to wood moldings are preformed urethane or polymer moldings. These synthetic products are an especially good choice for highly detailed trim, such as an elaborate crown molding, which covers the joint between the walls and ceiling. In many cases, the synthetic molding is cheaper than wood, and some styles are available with pre-formed corner pieces, which saves do-it-yourselfers from having to make tricky compound-angle cuts where the molding meets at the corners.

Metal Panels

Pressed-steel panels used for "tin" ceilings are an increasingly popular choice for kitchen surfaces. They're available in a wide variety of modern and traditional patterns. Copper, brass and chrome panels are also available, but at double or triple the price of steel. You can paint the panels to match your decor, or combine patterns to create a custom look. Installing the panels requires careful layout, but it's not too difficult for most experienced do-it-yourselfers.

Mirrors & Glass Block

The light-enhancing properties of mirrors and glass block offer an excellent way to make a small kitchen look bigger and brighter. For example, you might cover your entire backsplash with mirrors or convert part of a non-load-bearing wall to glass block. The smaller mirrors that you can buy at home centers are easy to install yourself, but it's best to contact a glazier for any mirror that's larger than 2 × 3 ft. or that must be custom-cut.

■ *The patterned glass panels on this backsplash create a reflective surface that magnifies the under-cabinet lighting.*

SOURCES

Beyond Paint & Wallpaper

A.A. Abbingdon (metal panels): 718/258-8333

CDM (preformed molding): 800/543-0553; www.custom-moulding.com

Chicago Metallic (metal panels): 800/323-7164; www.chicagometallic.com

Cultured Stone: 800/255-1727; www.culturedstone.com

Eldorado Stone: 800/925-1491; www.eldoradostone.com

Flex Trim (preformed molding): 800/356-9060; www.flextrim.com

Focal Point (preformed molding & paneling): 800/662-5550; www.focalpointap.com

Fypon (polymer molding): 800/537-5349; www.fypon.com

Haida (cedar paneling): 604/437-3434; www.haidaforest.com

International Glass Block: 323/585-6368; www.glassblockco.com

Nu-Wood (preformed molding): 800/526-1278; www.nu-wood.com

Outwater Plastics (preformed molding): 800/789-5322; www.outwater.com

Pittsburgh Corning (glass block): 800/624-2120; www.pittsburghcorning.com

RAS Industries (preformed molding): 800/367-1076

Style-Mark (preformed molding): 800/446-3040; www.style-mark.com

Weck Glass Block: 815/356-8440; www.glashaus.com

W.F. Norman (metal panels): 417/667-5552

Designing with Flooring

From a design standpoint, flooring is far more than the surface you walk on and mop up. Designers and remodelers routinely use flooring to alter the way a room looks and works; with a little planning, you can reap the same benefits. A custom-designed floor can be a cost-efficient solution to an awkward kitchen floor plan—it can help unify a complicated layout, highlight an interesting focal point or direct traffic away from specific appliances and work areas.

Before you decide on a flooring material, consider the possibilities of designing with flooring. Think of your floor as a big canvas and your flooring as the paint. You can design with almost any kind of flooring, including sheet vinyl, vinyl tile squares, ceramic tile, laminate flooring and wood strips or planks. The only difference is that instead of using just one color or pattern, you design inset shapes or borders to accomplish your design goals. You can use the following principles with any flooring, as long as you keep in mind the limitations of the materials you've selected.

Using Visual Tricks

First, examine your kitchen and determine what you're trying to accomplish. Do you want to redirect traffic, highlight a focal point, unify a fragmented room or make the room look bigger, wider or longer? Here are some visual tricks you can use to accomplish these goals.

• To make a square room look more dynamic and interesting, divide it into large triangles of color (Illustration A, page 121).

• To make a narrow galley kitchen appear wider, run a series of wide horizontal "ladder" stripes perpendicular to the long walls (B).

• To make a short kitchen look longer, run narrow stripes of contrasting colors parallel to the long walls.

• To unify a kitchen that has many jogs, nooks and crannies, create a perimeter border that fills in the deviations and draws a straight line along an inner color (C).

• To make a large room look smaller, use two or more bold, contrasting colors.

• To make a small room look bigger, use no more than two light, cool, low-contrast colors (such as off-white and beige, or white and pale blue).

• To fill in a large open space, set several increasingly smaller squares inside one another, or place a patterned square inside a solid-color square (or vice versa). You could also place the color field on a diagonal, or define it with intersecting diamonds (D).

• To redirect traffic, use borders to mark the pathways.

You can draw attention (and traffic) to a built-in island or breakfast bar by highlighting the floor around it. For example, if the floor has a perimeter border, repeat it around the island. If the floor is plain, surround the island with a strong color. Another approach is to create an "area rug" around the island in an

■ *The area rug design on this floor draws the eye to the unique shape of the island.*

accent color. You can use the same technique to set off a kitchen dining area. For example, anchor a breakfast table and chairs in a colored square or rectangle, then surround it with a 2-in.-wide border in a third color.

When selecting colors and shapes, you might repeat the lines of other elements in the room, such as an archway or a cornice curve. Or, you can reproduce any shape that appeals to you, such as a favorite detail from a quilt pattern. To gather floor design ideas, collect photographs from home improvement books and magazines.

Creating a Design

Once you've defined your goals, draw a scaled floor plan of your kitchen on graph paper and make several copies of it (see **Create Your Drawings**, pages 46-47). Use the drawings to experiment with patterns and colors. To see how a pattern will look in the room, borrow flooring samples and tape them to the floor. This can help you decide whether you prefer a bold color contrast or a more subtle effect.

Finally, cut your design out of colored paper and secure it to the floor with masking tape. Check it from several angles and fine tune the details: Should the border be thicker or thinner? Is the pattern too busy?

Determining the Cost

Custom designed floors are relatively expensive; for example, even a simple design can double the cost of a sheet vinyl floor. However, if the new floor can transform your awkward kitchen and make it work better, it's bound to be a far less expensive solution than rearranging the layout of the room.

The final cost will depend on your flooring material, the complexity of your design, the size and shape of your room and the condition of your existing floor. Also, in this case it may not be advisable to save money by installing the flooring yourself—with sheet vinyl, for example, one slip of the knife can ruin the entire floor.

As a rule, the more colors or patterns in your plan, the more costly the floor will be. To find out what the new floor will cost, take your sketch to a flooring store. The dealer can help you determine the cost and, if necessary, modify the design to fit your budget.

■ *Four ways to design with flooring:*
A. Divide a square room into large triangles of color.
B. "Widen" a narrow room with ladder stripes.
C. Use a solid border to "simplify" a busy layout.
D. Fill in an open space with intersecting diamonds.

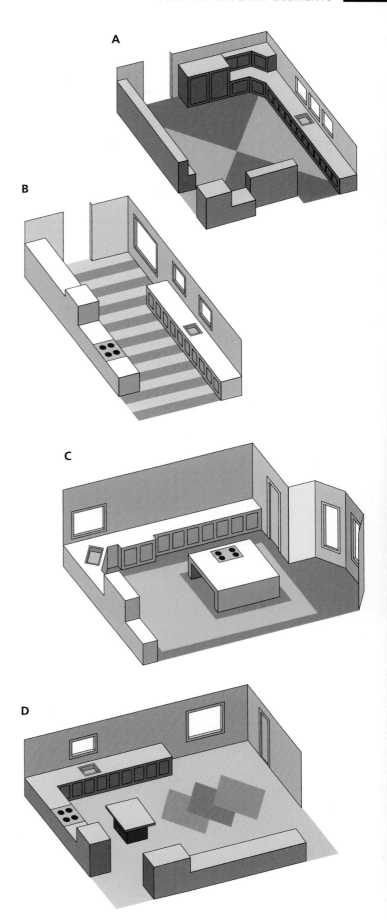

A

B

C

D

Resilient Flooring

Resilient flooring is both the least expensive material you can use to cover your kitchen floor and the easiest and quickest to install. In addition to being durable and easy to clean, it's available in a wide range of colors, as well as in patterns that mimic the look of ceramic tile, natural stone, marble, brick and wood.

Shopping for Quality

Resilient flooring varies widely in durability and price—sheet vinyl, for example, ranges between $10 and $45 per sq. yd. The three major categories of vinyl flooring are solid vinyl (PVC), vinyl composites and printed flooring. In general, the more vinyl a flooring has, the more durable and cushioned it will be, and the more it will cost.

The quality of resilient flooring has improved greatly over the last several years. Cushioned backings, upgraded warranties and guaranteed moisture and mildew protection are now common features. However, as these features have been added, the price of top-quality vinyl flooring has climbed to the level of tile and hardwood.

Solid vinyl flooring is the best quality (although the name is deceiving; it may contain as little as 40 percent PVC). It's composed of vinyl granules embedded in a vinyl base. During manufacturing, the granules puff up to cushion the floor. Some products also incorporate chips of quartz or granite for a more natural look.

Vinyl composites are generally considered to be standard vinyl flooring. These are created by fusing colored vinyl with non-vinyl fillers. Many better-quality resilient flooring products are vinyl composites. Printed flooring is the lowest in cost and quality; it's composed of non-vinyl materials that are coated with a protective layer.

Thickness is another clue to quality. Thicker flooring is more comfortable and puncture-resistant, since it generally includes more vinyl. Solid-vinyl gets most of its thickness from its vinyl core. With vinyl composite and printed flooring, additional thickness comes from the *wear layer*—a coating of clear vinyl. All three types are topped with a thinner, protective layer. There's a direct correlation between the quality of a floor's wear layer and the amount of maintenance it requires (again, thicker is better). The material used for the top layer varies among manufacturers, but the better products typically include some type of urethane.

Choosing a Flooring

If you're shopping for resilient flooring, you'll need to choose between sheet vinyl and vinyl tiles; however, in a kitchen, this choice is fairly clear. Vinyl tiles are easy to install, and many come with peel-and-stick adhesive backing. But since the floor ends up with a lot of seams, moisture can easily seep in between the tiles and ruin the bond. For this reason, sheet vinyl tile is a much better choice for a kitchen floor.

Sheet vinyl can be installed in two ways: *full-spread* and *perimeter-bond*. Perimeter-bond vinyl has a vinyl backing and is easier to install, since it's glued down only at its seams and edges. Full-spread vinyl has a felt or paper backing

■ *Sheet vinyl flooring can mimic the look of glazed ceramic tiles.*

and is installed over a coat of adhesive spread over the entire floor. In most kitchens, full-spread vinyl is the best choice. Perimeter-bond vinyl was developed to be installed over existing vinyl floors, and is able to disguise minor imperfections in the surface; select it only if this is a major issue in your kitchen.

Sheet vinyl comes in 6-, 9- and 12-ft. widths that are cut to fit the floor space. Although the 6-ft. width is the easiest to manage and the most economical, it's not the best choice for most kitchen floors, where it's important to minimize the number of seams. If your floor must have a seam, place it as far as possible from the sink, dishwasher or other water source.

Installing it Yourself

If you want to install resilient flooring yourself, select a product with a warranty that allows do-it-yourself installation. For full-spread vinyl, you'll need to nail, screw or staple a new plywood underlayment to the subfloor and fill all the holes and seams with patching compound. Check the manufacturer's installation specifications, as some will void the warranty if their flooring is installed over a substandard underlayment.

To protect your new flooring while you move the kitchen appliances and furniture back into place, cover it with hardboard panels until everything is set.

■ *Full-spread vinyl flooring is glued onto a plywood underlayment that's attached to the subfloor. The underlayment must be smooth and solid to ensure a quality job.*

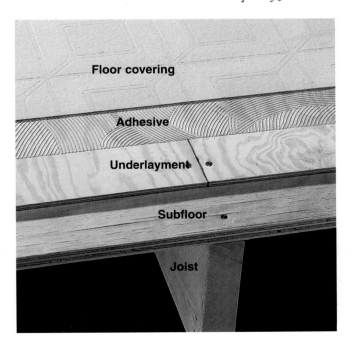

Floor covering

Adhesive

Underlayment

Subfloor

Joist

SOURCES

Resilient Flooring

AMTICO: 800-268-4260; www.amtico.com
ARMSTRONG (LINOLEUM, OTHERS): 800/233-3823; www.armstrong.com
CONGOLEUM: 800/274-2366; www.congoleum.com
DOMCO (VINYL & LINOLEUM): 800/227-4662; www.domco.com
FORBO (LINOLEUM): 800/342-0604; www.forbo.com
HOBOKEN WOOD FLOORING (LINOLEUM): 800/222-1068
MANNINGTON: 609/339-5848; www.mannington.com
PROTECTIVE PRODUCTS: 800-789-6633; www.protective-products.com

Ceramic Tile Flooring

Ceramic tile is the hardest, most durable flooring you can install in your kitchen. It's an excellent option for kitchen floors because it can withstand heavy traffic, impact and moisture and is easy to clean up with soap and water. In addition, tile offers almost limitless opportunities to customize the design of your floor.

The drawbacks of ceramic tile are that it can be cold, slippery, noisy and hard to stand on for long periods of time. Because it's so hard, anything fragile that falls on the floor is likely to break. However, most of these problems can be minimized by adding accent and area rugs to your kitchen.

Buying Floor Tile

You can find more information on ceramic tile by turning to **Ceramic Tile Countertops**, on pages 92-93. The best choice of tile for kitchen floors and countertops is floor tile, but there are different considerations for each application. Because counters cover a smaller area than a floor, you're likely to use relatively smaller tiles there— perhaps 4 in. to 6 in. tile, whereas a common tile size for a floor is 12 in. And while the tile used for both areas should be glazed, floors need greater hardness for durability and some slip resistance. You can get this with a textured or "soft-glazed" tile (just ask the salesperson about the tile's slip-resistance rating).

All floor tile must bear the burden of foot traffic, but not all types can stand up to the demands placed on a kitchen floor. For kitchens, tile manufacturers recommend using tile with a Class (or Group) 3, 4 or 5 rating.

■ *Some ceramic tiles closely mimic the irregular coloring and texture of natural stone.*

(Class 2 tile is suitable for most bathroom floors, but it isn't hard enough for kitchens.) If there's no Class rating, look for floor tile that is rated for commercial use.

The best places to buy floor tile are stores that specialize in tile or floor coverings, which usually have a better selection than home centers. A good tile store will have experts on staff who can give you sound advice on color, layout and technical issues.

Before you decide on a tile, take a few different samples home and lay them down on your kitchen floor. Check the colors of the tile against the countertops and appliances.

Installing Floor Tile

Hiring a professional to tile your new floor can be expensive—between $3 and 5$ per sq. ft.—but it's usually worth the expense. Creating a pleasing layout takes an eye for the geometry of the entire room, and many layouts involve numerous cut tiles, which are difficult to get right. If you decide to install your own tile, be aware that a successful tile job involves careful preparation of the floor and the proper combination of materials. For more information about installing floor tile in your kitchen, contact the Tile Council of America (see page 155).

Here's an idea of what's involved in a typical tile installation, starting with the floor's structural supports.

• *Subfloor.* The subfloor is the structural skin that covers the floor joists (see page 123); this may be $^3/_4$-in.-thick plywood or oriented strand board (OSB) or 1 × 6 planks. Whatever the material, the subfloor must be flat and stiff. A subfloor that flexes too much must be stiffened with additional joists, an extra layer of plywood or both.

• *Substrate.* The substrate goes on top of the subfloor and is the surface to which the tile adheres. In some

professional installations, the substrate is a thick mortar bed reinforced with wire mesh. However, many do-it-yourselfers use a cementitious backer board for a tile substrate, because it's easier to install (it's also thinner than a mortar bed). This should be glued and screwed to the subfloor, and all of its seams should be taped and filled with thinset mortar (see below).

• *Adhesive.* The adhesive used to secure the tile must be compatible with the tile and substrate, but the most common adhesive for floor tile is called *thinset.* It comes in a dry powder that you mix with water. Pre-mixed organic adhesives are generally not recommended for floors.

• *Sealer.* There are two types of sealer—one is for tile, the other for grout; both types are clear liquids that prevent stains. If you're using unglazed tile, such as quarry tile, you must apply a tile sealer after the tile is set and before it is grouted. Grout sealer is necessary on any grout other than epoxy grout, which seals itself. Apply grout sealer after the new grout has cured fully.

• *Grout.* Grout is a cement-based mortar that fills the spaces between individual tiles and creates a watertight seal. Epoxy grout is inherently stain-resistant and is best for kitchen floors; however, it can be difficult to work with. Standard grouts should be mixed with a latex additive to add stain resistance.

■ *Left: This floor combines several different tile sizes in a well-balanced layout.*

■ *Above: Dark handmade ceramic tile insets are the focal point of this kitchen.*

SOURCES

Ceramic Tile Flooring

AMERICAN OLEAN: 800/268-8453; www.aotile.com
ANN SACKS TILE & STONE: 503/281-7751; www.annsacks.com
CROSSVILLE CERAMICS: 615/484-2110; www.crossvilleceramics.com
DALTILE: 800/933-8453; www.daltile.com
FLORIDA TILE INDUSTRIES: 800/789-8453; www.fltile.com
INTERCERAMIC USA: 800/496-8453; www.interceramicusa.com
LAUFEN CERAMIC TILE: 800/758-8453; www.laufen.com
SENECA TILES: 800/426-4335
SONOMA TILEMAKERS: 707/837-8177; www.sonomatilemakers.com
SUMMITVILLE TILES: 330/223-1511; www.summitville.com
TILECERA: 800/388-8905
TILEMAKERS: 770/434-6100; www.tilemakers.com
UNITED STATES CERAMIC TILE: 800/321-0684; www.usceramictileco.com

■ *The "photo" layer of this laminate flooring is based on planks from antique oak barn floors.*

ers topped with a finish that resists scratches and stains; however, there are some key differences between the two. Consider these points to help you decide:

• Does your floor take lots of abuse from children or pets? If so, choose plastic laminate or acrylic-finished wood laminate; they're the toughest.

• Do you want a natural wood look? If so, choose wood laminate; its top layer is wood veneer, so it looks and feels the most like solid-wood strip or plank flooring.

• Will the added height of the new flooring create an awkward transition between rooms? If so, choose plastic laminates; they're the thinnest.

Wood Laminate Flooring

Wood laminates are available in tongue-and-groove planks of varying widths. The planks are similar in construction to plywood. Thin plies of wood are glued together to create a strong, uniform sheet. Then, a top layer of wood veneer is added to give the appearance of solid wood. As with solid-wood strip flooring, oak is the best-selling wood laminate. Other popular species are maple and cherry. All come prefinished in a variety of colors.

Wood laminates have either a polyurethane surface finish or an acrylic-impregnated finish. For a polyurethane finish, the wood is stained, then seven or eight layers of finish are applied over it. Warranties for polyurethane finishes usually range from two to five years.

The acrylic system is more thorough. A liquid acrylic is colored and then injected into the wood. It penetrates the entire first layer and solidifies, creating a composite of wood and plastic. The result is a tougher finish, a longer warranty (up to 25 years) and sometimes even a commercial rating. However, acrylic-finished products also cost a bit more.

Professional installation of wood laminates costs about as much as for a solid-wood floor, but the process is far easier; many wood laminate products are marketed to the do-it-yourselfer. Although the installation usually

Two Kinds of "Laminate" Flooring

Laminate flooring refers to two relatively new flooring options: wood laminate, or "engineered products," and plastic laminate. Both types are available in styles that closely mimic solid-wood strip or plank flooring. Although neither can be sanded and refinished like solid-wood flooring, they offer some distinct advantages over their solid-wood counterparts. Laminate products are generally easier to install than solid-wood, and with most types there are at least two installation options. One option allows you to lay laminate flooring over old floor coverings, as well as over concrete. Laminates can also save you money, as prices for many laminate products end where prices for better-quality solid-wood flooring begin.

Both wood and plastic laminates consist of bonded lay-

isn't complicated, you'll need solid do-it-yourself skills and preferably some experience laying floors. Bear in mind that hiring a professional may be well worth it if your kitchen is large, you're short on time or the job requires lots of complicated cuts. In any case, make sure to store the flooring in the room where it will be installed for at least 48 hours prior to installation. This allows the wood to adjust to the ambient humidity level so it doesn't shrink or expand after it's been laid.

You can install wood laminate flooring just like solid-wood strips—that is nail or staple it to a plywood sub-floor. Another method involves gluing each piece to the subfloor. A third installation option, known as the "floating floor" method, is by far the most versatile. With this method, the tongue-and-groove edges of the planks are glued together to form one piece that "floats" on top of a special foam pad. Because a floating floor isn't secured to its substrate, it can be used on almost any flat interior surface. However, installations over surfaces that may produce moisture, such as a concrete slab, require a plastic vapor barrier beneath the foam pad.

With any of the above installations, be sure to leave a ¹⁄₂-in. gap between the flooring and all of the walls, to allow room for the flooring to expand. Use base molding and base shoe to cover the gaps. Also, use only the adhesive and installation procedures recommended by the manufacturer, or you may void the warranty.

Plastic Laminate Flooring

Plastic laminates are made with a medium-density fiberboard (MDF) core topped with a layer of plastic laminate similar to the material used on countertops (but about ten times denser). Like the countertop material, the laminate has a photographic image, or "photo," layer that can mimic wood, stone and many other materials, as well as display a solid color. The laminate is topped with a thick layer of clear melamine, making it extremely durable and resistant to scuffs and stains.

Plastic laminates are available in dozens of colors and patterns, in both tongue-and-groove planks and tiles. Plastic laminate tiles are sometimes glued down, while the planks are typically installed as a floating floor.

■ *The design of this plastic laminate flooring perfectly suits the rustic look of this eating area.*

SOURCES

Laminate Flooring

ARMSTRONG: 800/233-3823; www.armstrong.com
BHK: 800/663-4176; www.bhkofamerica.com
BRUCE LAMINATE FLOORS: 800/722-4647;
www.brucehardwoodfloors.com
FORMICA: 800/367-6422; www.formica.com
MANNINGTON FLOORS: 800/443-5667;
www. mannington.com
NEVAMAR: 800/638-4380; www.nevamar.com
PERGO: 800/337-3746; www.pergo.com
PIONITE: 800/746-6483; www.pionitelaminates.com
TARKETT: 800/842-7816; www.tarkettna.com
WILSONART: 800/433-3222; www.wilsonart.com

Solid-Wood Flooring

Solid-wood flooring is a traditional favorite that's fast gaining popularity in kitchens. It not only looks inviting, but feels warm, too, which can be an important consideration in chilly climates. However, before you select solid wood flooring for your kitchen floor, you need to understand its advantages and disadvantages.

Although solid wood is not as hard or abrasion-resistant as tile or stone, it can be refinished, and that gives it a longer life than most flooring materials. An expert wood finisher can stain your new wood flooring to match the other woodwork in your house, such as your kitchen cabinetry or the flooring in adjacent rooms. In addition, solid wood is a resilient material that's very comfortable to stand on for long periods.

The most notable disadvantage to wood flooring is that it's vulnerable to water damage; in a kitchen, that's a significant drawback. If your wood floor has a good finish, you can avoid most water damage by wiping up spills as soon as possible. However, a leak from a sink or a dishwasher that goes unnoticed for a while can cause

irreversible damage. A wood floor also requires more careful maintenance than other floor coverings. If you're used to slopping a wet mop over your old vinyl or tile floor, you may find the frequent sweeping and careful damp-mopping necessary with a wood floor to be inconvenient.

What's underneath the floor is also an important consideration. A solid-wood floor must be installed over a flat, dry subfloor. If your kitchen floor lies over a damp crawl space, heating pipes or uninsulated ductwork, lay down a vapor barrier and use laminated flooring rather than solid-wood (see pages 126-127).

Selecting Wood Flooring

Solid-wood flooring is available in wide planks, narrow strips and parquet squares. Planks and strips are typically $3/4$-in. thick, and the most common type by far is the familiar $2 1/4$-in.-wide tongue-and-groove strip. The cost of this type varies according to the type and grade of the wood. Red and white oak are the most common and affordable. Red oak begins around $2.25 per square foot (material only), and white oak runs slightly more. Suitable alternatives to oak include maple, ash, beech and hickory. Avoid using pine and other softwoods in your kitchen, as they're less resistant to dents and scratches.

You'll also find different grades of flooring within each wood species. *Select* and *clear* grades are made from premium, knot-free boards. *Common* and *#2* grades are less expensive and will show more variation in grain and color, as well as occasional tight knots. To save money, you can ask for shorter strips, or "shorts." However, shorter pieces will create a busier-looking floor with more end joints. Another way to reduce your cost is to look for sale prices, since wood flooring is frequently discounted.

Several manufacturers offer solid wood flooring that comes with a factory-applied finish. Although this increases the price of the flooring, it's a good option for remodeling, since it eliminates the sawdust involved in sanding the floor and the fumes involved in staining and finishing it. The factory finishes are generally high quality and very durable.

■ *As a flooring material that's suitable for many rooms of the house, solid wood is perfect for linking the kitchen with an adjoining eating area.*

Installing & Finishing

Installing solid-wood strip flooring is a fairly straightforward process. It all starts with a clean, sound subfloor, over which a layer of building paper is laid. This protects the subfloor from water damage and prevents squeaking. The strips are nailed to the subfloor, one-at-a-time, by means of a hammer-operated or pneumatic nailer. 1/2-in. to 3/4-in. expansion gaps are left at all the walls.

With prefinished flooring, the installation is complete as soon as all the strips are nailed down and the base molding is installed. Unfinished flooring, however, must be sanded smooth with powerful sanding machines, then finished to protect the wood. If you're getting new cabinets, it's a good idea to have unfinished flooring installed and sanded before the cabinets go in.

The standard finish for kitchen floors is polyurethane. Available in oil- and water-based formulations, polyurethane forms a durable clear layer that seals the top of the wood.

An experienced do-it-yourselfer can rent a nailer and install a prefinished floor with little trouble, but an unfinished floor is a different story; a novice can easily damage a floor with a drum sander, and it can be difficult to apply an even finish over an entire floor. For most homeowners, a professional installation is worth the cost: about $2 to $3 per sq. ft.

Maintaining it Well

Because dirt abrades the finish, the best thing you can do for your wood floor is sweep or vacuum it frequently. When it needs more thorough cleaning, mist the floor with a non-oily, non-ammonia cleaner or a light vinegar-and-water-solution, and wipe it with a slightly damp mop or a broom wrapped in toweling. Be careful with cleaners. Soaps and detergents that leave an oily residue may make it impossible to re-coat the floor. Your flooring or finish manufacturer will probably recommend a detergent that you can use for damp-mopping. Never use wax on a polyurethane floor.

Re-coating a polyurethane floor is a maintenance procedure that involves "screening" the floor with a buffer screen so that a new coat of polyurethane can adhere to the existing finish. This is different from refinishing the floor, which involves removing the old finish and a thin layer of wood with sanding machines before a new finish is applied. Re-coating does not remove deep scratches or other damage; it should be done every two years or so.

■ *A solid-wood floor stained to match the cabinets can create a warm feeling and unify all the elements of the room.*

SOURCES

Solid Wood Flooring

ANDERSON HARDWOOD FLOORS: 800/252-4186; www.andersonfloors.com.
BRUCE HARDWOOD FLOORS: 800/722-4647; www.brucehardwoodfloors.com.
HARRIS-TARKETT: 800/842-7816; www.harristarkett.com
HARTCO: 423/569-8888; www.hartcoflooring.com
MANNINGTON FLOORS: 800/443-5667; www. mannington.com
PREMIER WOOD FLOORS: 800/722-4647
ROBBINS HARDWOOD FLOORS: 800/733-3309; www.robbinsflooring.com
HARDWOOD FINISHES:
FLECTO: 510/655-2470; www.verathane.com
MINWAX: 800/523-9299; www.minwax.com
VALSPAR: 800/323-5129; www.valspar.com
WILLIAM ZINSSER: 732/469-8100; www.zinsser.com

LIGHTING, WINDOWS & SKYLIGHTS

A comfortable and efficient kitchen requires a combination of natural and artificial light sources, carefully integrated with your overall design scheme to create well-lighted work areas as well as an inviting place for your family and friends to gather. Although most kitchens have some kind of natural light source, they also require good artificial lighting. Light fixtures should direct the right amount of illumination to the right places for all your activities, including food preparation, dining and cleanup. Good lighting ensures your safety when handling hot pans, sharp knives and wet utensils, and helps make cooking and cleanup enjoyable activities rather than dreary

chores. The right lights also add a distinctive touch of sparkle that gives life to a room and makes it memorable.

Windows and skylights are a kitchen's main source of natural light, but they perform other essential functions, as well. A window's design and its treatment can add personality and charm to a room, while its shape and placement allow you to direct light where it's needed. By breaking up walls and ceilings, windows and skylights can expand a room's perceived boundaries, making it appear larger.

The right windows and window treatments also help ensure your comfort in all seasons by letting you control the flow of warmth, light and fresh air into your kitchen from outdoors. When choosing windows, it's important to consider your needs for privacy and energy efficiency, as well as the visual effect that the windows will have on the exterior of your home.

■ *Opposite: The combination of natural lighting provided by stylishly shaded windows and artificial lighting offered by decorative pendant fixtures makes this kitchen a welcoming place at any time of day.* ■ *Above: Coordinated countertop fixtures ensure plentiful task lighting for safe, enjoyable meal preparation.*

Kitchen Lighting

Good lighting can change the way a room feels as well as the way you feel about the room. In fact, improving the lighting is the major impetus behind many kitchen remodeling projects. When you visit a home where the kitchen somehow just feels natural and "right," you can bet there's a carefully-designed lighting scheme behind it.

Creating a Lighting Plan

A good lighting plan employs each of the main types of lighting—*ambient, task* and *accent*—to its best effect. To begin creating a plan, sketch the room and indicate all current sources of light, including all natural light. Next, make a list of the tasks that typically are done in your kitchen and note where each task is done and by whom. Finally, consider the three main types of lighting and imagine how you might use each of them to provide effective, attractive light for those daily tasks.

Ambient Lighting

Ambient light is the background illumination that suffuses a room, both natural and artificial. Ideally, it should come from several subtle light sources that cast little shadow or glare—such as that provided by sunlight on an overcast day, or overhead fixtures. Standard ceiling-mounted fixtures are the most common way to enhance a room's natural ambient light, however there are other options. Recessed canister fixtures, which are sleek and unobtrusive, are popular. Track lighting is adjustable and allows you to add more ambient light where you need it most. Square fluorescent lights, an energy-efficient form of ambient light, don't cast harsh shadows.

Current trends in ambient lighting include techniques referred to as *wall washing* and *indirect lighting*. Wall washing involves placing lights at regular intervals to

■ *Recessed canister light fixtures are an excellent, stylish way to create a warm ambient glow in a kitchen.*

■ *Above: The task lighting over a work area can also highlight its decorative elements, such as this terra cotta backsplash.*

■ *Right: Accent lighting should be used sparingly to draw the eye to featured spots, such as this elegant orchid.*

illuminate walls or ceilings evenly. Indirect lighting uses the surfaces of a room as reflectors, neutrally distributing glare-free ambient light.

Task Lighting

Task lighting illuminates the work areas used for cooking and food preparation; in a kitchen, task lighting is critical. Overhead fixtures make poor task lights in areas of the kitchen with wall cabinets. And because most kitchen work areas are located on the perimeter of the room, your body usually blocks the light from a centrally located overhead fixture, putting your work surface in shadow.

Good sources of task lighting typically include under-cabinet fixtures or track lights placed so the beam falls on the counter in front of you as you work. Hanging lights can also provide good task illumination. In addition, they serve the design function of breaking up the horizontal lines of the kitchen cabinets and counters.

Accent Lighting

Accent lighting typically is used to highlight artwork or interesting architectural features. Because it needs to be precisely controlled, accent lighting typically is comprised of lower-voltage, directional light sources operated by independent switches.

Experiment with placement and combinations of light sources to achieve dramatic effects. For instance, a white halogen light can create a spotlight effect in a room suffused with warm incandescent light.

■ *This kitchen effectively combines recessed fixtures that provide ambient light and under-cabinet fixtures that illuminate the work areas, casting a warm glow over the tile backsplash.*

Saving Energy

Since lighting accounts for 12 to 15 percent of the typical electric bill, it's wise to educate yourself about the energy efficiency of the lighting fixtures you're considering and the overall plan you're creating.

Light the room appropriately, but not beyond what's necessary—reducing wattage reduces energy consumption. In areas that need to be brightly lit, you can save energy by using a single high-wattage bulb rather than several low-wattage bulbs. For instance, one 100-watt bulb produces about the same amount of light as two 60-watt bulbs, but it costs less to operate. Lighting controls can help you save energy, too. For example, use dimmer switches where your lighting needs are variable, such as over a kitchen eating area.

And since natural light is the cheapest of all, try to place task areas under windows or skylights, and magnify the brightness of the room by using light colors on finishes, surfaces and walls.

Fluorescent bulbs are the most efficient source of artificial light; although they may cost more initially, they

---

TIP

Lighting Lingo: Bulb Types

Incandescent: The common lightbulb. Inefficient but reliable, the primary source of light in most homes.
Fluorescent: Fluorescent lamps burn cooler, last longer and are cheaper to operate than incandescent and halogen bulbs. They produce much less heat than incandes-

cent bulbs, and can be just as effective at making colors and skin tones look good.
Halogen: Halogen lights operate in basically the same way as incandescent bulbs, but they contain halogen gas, which creates a much brighter glow.

can save you 60 percent over incandescent bulbs and will last 13 times longer. Halogen bulbs also last longer than incandescents and generate 30 percent more light from the same amount of electricity.

Finally, consider the building codes that apply in your area. For example, in California, the codes require that the primary fixtures in kitchens be fluorescent.

Lighting a Kitchen

The objective in a kitchen is to provide plenty of light while minimizing glare and shadows. Start with ambient light, then add task and accent lighting to illuminate specific areas according to the way you and your family use the kitchen.

Counters & Work Areas

Countertops can be effectively illuminated with fluorescent strips or halogen "hockey pucks" hidden under the cabinets. A 50-watt halogen bulb will illuminate up to 48 in. of countertop. Thin-profile fluorescent fixtures come in many lengths and wattages, but they can't be dimmed. If your countertops are shiny, angle the light toward the backsplash or install a light shield.

At the sink, you might use a recessed ceiling light that can be directed where the light is needed. With a dimmer switch, this fixture can also provide a nice glow when you don't need full illumination. When installing recessed lighting above countertops, place the fixtures 24 to 36 in. away from the wall and 36 to 48 in. apart.

The most common way to provide task lighting for a cooktop is a range hood with an integral bulb. If you need more light, add an overhead fixture.

To create accent lighting along cabinets and work areas, you can place lighting strips along the top or base of the kitchen cabinets, or add indirect lighting from fixtures aimed toward the walls or ceiling.

Islands

Above islands, bright halogen pendant lights are quite

■ *Pendant lights add a vertical design element and provide good task lighting for islands and counters.*

effective. The bottom of the fixture should be 30 in. above the work surface. If you're adding pot racks, position them carefully to avoid casting shadows.

Eating Areas

In eating areas, a hanging fixture over the table is the traditional choice. However, you can also use multiple recessed lights and wall sconces to create atmosphere and provide enough light for doing paperwork.

Pantries

In a pantry, fluorescent lighting works well; the bulbs last a long time and they're energy efficient. However, codes require that the fixture have a glass or plastic cover.

SOURCES

Lighting

ASPEN LIGHTING: 800/455-4680; www.aspenlighting.com
CASELLA LIGHTING: 415/626-9600; www.casellalighting.com
INTERMATIC LIGHTING: 815/675-2321; www.intermatic.com
LIGHTOLIER: 508/679-8131; www.lightolier.com
OUTWATER PLASTICS: 800/543-3217; www.outwater.com

PROGRESS LIGHTING: 864/599-6000; www.progresslighting.com
THOMAS LIGHTING: 800/825-5844; www.thomaslighting.com
W.A.C. LIGHTING: 800/526-2588; www.waclighting.com

Designing with Windows

Windows can have a dramatic impact on the appeal and livability of your kitchen. By shaping the flow of natural light and fresh air into the room, the windows help determine how comfortable your kitchen will be to use and how all its colors, textures and finishes will look once they're in place.

The brainstorming phase of planning your new kitchen is the time to consider how various window design options might alter or enhance the room. Since different kinds of windows offer different benefits, the first step in choosing the right windows for your kitchen is determining and prioritizing your design goals.

There are four primary benefits you can gain by replacing windows: adding more sunlight, ventilating the room, framing a view and defining a space. The suggestions that follow will help you select a window design that will enhance your kitchen and achieve the results you're looking for.

Adding Light

Many of us dream of a bright, sunny kitchen, suffused with the warm glow of natural light. If abundant natural light is your primary goal, bear in mind that light from a typical window penetrates into a space two and half times the height of the window's opening. The one exception is a band of clerestory windows (windows high along the top of a wall) which can carry light deeper into a room.

The amount, angle and quality of the sunlight you'll receive will vary considerably, depending on the window's orientation. A southern window is the best source for warm ambient light; a northern opening will provide cool indirect light. An eastern window will admit morning light, while a west-facing window will let in the strong afternoon sun.

■ *This bay window over the sink provides a sunny spot for plants and a lovely view that makes cleanup a pleasure.*

■ *An alcove window, such as this striking stained-glass panel, can be an eye-catching feature above a kitchen sink.*

When planning your windows, check to see if there are any trees that may block the sun. If so, determine how they'll affect the light throughout the seasons: check the path of the summer and winter sun, and note whether the trees lose their leaves in winter.

Also, don't forget to consider the color of your kitchen walls. Light tones will reflect sunlight, making the room appear brighter; dark tones will have the opposite effect.

Ventilating a Room

To improve a room's ventilation, consider crank-open casement windows; they allow you to regulate and direct air circulation most effectively. To shield your kitchen from strong sunlight during certain hours of the day, install retractable awnings.

Another cooling idea is to create cross ventilation by placing windows on opposite walls. To maximize the air flow, keep the windows away from the corners. To increase the velocity and cooling power of the cross-breeze, have the air enter through a smaller window and exit through a larger one.

Framing a View

If you're trying to show off a striking vista, your first impulse may be to install a sweeping picture window. However, you'll soon discover that a really big expanse of glass costs really big money. Also, integrating a picture window into an existing wall takes up a lot of precious wall space and requires some expensive structural changes.

Instead, consider grouping several smaller windows a few inches apart. In addition to saving money, this approach divides the view into more manageable visual elements. Since our eyes can only span about 60 degrees at a time, segmenting a view actually makes it more interesting and easier to appreciate.

Defining a Space

One of the best ways to define a kitchen nook or a breakfast area is to add a bay or bow window (see **Adding a Bay Window**, pages 142-143). However, you can also cluster regular windows to create a focal point or place a single fixed pane in a prominent position.

TIP

Window Design Tips

• Windows can be a good way to solve design problems. Check your kitchen for opportunities to add light and interest. For example, you may be able to transform a blank wall simply by adding an accent window.

• Bold window designs are best reserved for large spaces, such as two-story areas. Arched windows, round-top windows and pediment shapes will emphasize a room's height; banding windows together will accentuate its width.

• Don't be afraid to get creative with window trim. With wood-frame and clad wood windows, you can paint or stain the casing and interior portion of the frame to match the color of your cabinetry or trim. You'll also find casings and brickmolds in many different profiles. For added personal touches, use details such as corner blocks and keystones.

■ *These aluminum windows coordinate beautifully with the sleek metal finishes of the other surfaces in this kitchen.*

tractor for advice. It's generally best to choose window styles that complement the style of your home:

• Traditional homes (such as Cape Cod, Colonial or Victorian designs) look best with small double-hung "divided light" windows, which are referred to as "six-over-six" or "eight-over-eight"—the number of panes in each sash. For a unique touch, consider a cottage-style variation, where the bottom sash is taller and has larger panes than the top sash.

• Modern or contemporary style homes tend to look best with large metal-frame window units.

• Ranch-style homes are more adaptable. Although you can use divided lights, a contemporary design will generally look best with casement, slider and awning windows.

When installing windows, consider the sizes, positions and proportions of the windows carefully, so that they fit in with the other architectural elements of your home. For example, it's best to align the tops of all the windows in a straight line (typically 80 in. above the floor, level with the doors). Even if the windows are at different heights, positioning the tops along the same line will give both the interior and the exterior of your home a sense of order.

Buying Windows

Buying new windows is a big investment that requires careful planning. Whether your remodel involves replacing or redesigning existing windows or adding windows to an addition, you're bound to end up spending a lot of money. When buying windows, you need to select a window style, choose framing and glazing materials and compare energy efficiency ratings. You'll also find that several manufacturers offer a variety of decorative treatments, including beveled and stained glass panels.

Selecting a Style

When adding a window to a wall that already has windows, select a style that matches or is similar to that of the existing windows. If possible, gang windows together; a group of small windows generally looks better than one large unit.

If you don't like the window style you're replacing, look for alternate styles by studying other homes with styles similar to yours, or by asking a window dealer or con-

Choosing a Frame

When shopping for a window, you can start narrowing the options by choosing a frame material—vinyl, wood, clad wood, aluminum, fiberglass or composite. Here's a guide to the major frame materials.

Vinyl

Vinyl-frame windows are very affordable—as little as half as much as wood-frame windows—although not as pleasing aesthetically. However, they're energy efficient, never need repainting and can be made to fit any size opening (although your color options are somewhat limited). There is a wide range of quality. When shopping, look for a uniform color throughout the frame, extrusions that are stiff and thick-walled and joints that are heat-welded, rather than joined with screws or fasteners.

Wood

Although wood-frame windows have lost some of their market share to vinyl, they're still preferred by many professionals and homeowners. Wood-frame windows are strong, beautiful and relatively energy-efficient. Their primary disadvantage is that they must be periodically painted or refinished. When shopping for wood windows, look for easy operation and tight-fitting corners. Be sure any exposed wood is free of blemishes.

Clad Wood

Many manufacturers have addressed the maintenance issues of wood windows by cladding the window's exterior with vinyl or aluminum. The result is a tough, maintenance-free exterior and a natural wood interior that you can paint or stain. The major drawback with clad wood windows is that they usually cost more than wood windows.

Aluminum

Aluminum-frame windows, which were especially popular in the 1950s, offer the same durability, low cost and low maintenance advantages of vinyl. Their major drawback is reduced energy-efficiency—the metal frame conducts heat too easily. That makes aluminum frames feel cold to the touch and prone to condensation.

Those drawbacks make aluminum-frame windows suitable only for warm climates where cooling bills are greater than heating bills. If you opt for aluminum windows, be sure they have a *thermal break* in the frame—a strip of plastic or rubber that separates the inside and outside of the frame to limit heat conductivity.

Fiberglass & Composites

Fiberglass- and composite-frame windows are the newest options. Both are strong, maintenance-free and more energy-efficient than vinyl. At a price between vinyl and wood, they're affordable, and some of them can be painted to suit your taste.

As with vinyl windows, look for a uniform color throughout the frame and joints that are heat-welded rather than joined with fasteners.

The Anatomy of a Window

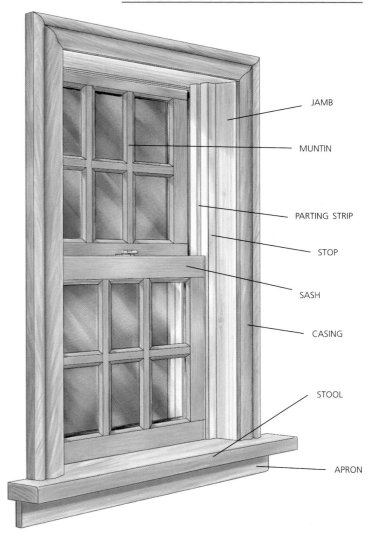

JAMB

MUNTIN

PARTING STRIP

STOP

SASH

CASING

STOOL

APRON

TIP

Code Compliance

When adding or enlarging windows, be sure to consider any state and local code restrictions that apply in your area. For example, in California (which has some of the most stringent codes in the country) you must have a total window area that's between 16 and 45 percent of the floor area of your home. The exact figure depends on a number of factors, including your climate, your heating, cooling and insulation systems and the U-value (page 140) of the windows.

■ *The shape and proportion of these gracefully arched windows complement the strong lines of this room.*

Glazing Options

In the not-so-distant past, the windows in most homes consisted of a single pane of glass. Glass by itself is a poor insulator, and in most regions, single-pane windows have contributed significantly to higher energy bills. But today's double-glazed windows can reduce the yearly energy cost in an average-size house by

hundreds of dollars.

Some of these savings come from two features that make double glazing more efficient: low-e coatings and inert gases between the panes. These features help stop heat loss or gain. While coated windows can be 10 to 15 percent more expensive than traditional windows, in most climates the added expense will be recouped by energy savings.

Rating Windows

A standard rating system developed by the National Fenestration Rating Council makes gauging the efficiency of a window quick and easy. Look for these ratings on each NFRC label:

• *U-value*: how much heat the window loses.
• *SHGC* (solar heat gain coefficient): how much heat the window lets in.
• *Visible light transmittance*: how much light the window lets in.

To cut winter energy loss in a cold climate, look for windows with a low U-value. To cut summer heat gain in a hot climate, look for units that have a low SHGC but still let in plenty of visible light.

An even simpler approach to finding efficient windows is to look for the government's Energy Star label, which identifies the most energy-efficient windows for specific climates. Windows that meet these energy requirements are 15 to 40 percent more efficient than those that simply meet typical code requirements. In a cold climate, Energy Star windows can have a U-value no higher than

---

TIP

Window Glazing Options

When buying windows, there are several glazing options you can choose from:
• Single-pane (A): suitable only for very mild climates.
• Double-pane (B): a sealed air space between the panes reduces heat loss. Double-panes are available in several variations to improve their insulating ability, including "low-e" glass (which has an invisible coating on one surface) and panes filled with an inert gas, such as argon.
• Double-glazed tinted glass (C): reduces heat buildup in southern climates.
• Tempered glass (D): required for patio doors and large picture windows.

■ *Windows can be used to form a transparent partition wall between two rooms.*

0.35. In a hot climate, they can have a U-value no higher than 0.75 and an SHGC no higher than 0.40. In mixed climates, they must have a U-value no higher than 0.40 and an SHGC no higher than 0.55.

Replacing Windows

Replacing windows no longer has to mean ripping out the entire window. There are three approaches you can take, depending on the condition of your old windows.

Sash Replacement

Many manufacturers offer kits that allow you to replace worn out sashes on double-hung windows. This job is done inside the house and won't disturb the interior or exterior trim. However, the new window must be the same style as the old one. Kits start at about $200, and are available in wood, vinyl or clad materials.

Frame Replacement

With this option, the existing stops and sash come out and a new window is placed in the old frame. (This is how most vinyl replacement windows are installed.) The windows can be made to the exact size of the opening, and you can change styles, provided the new unit fits the opening. Vinyl replacements cost about $250 to $300 installed. Wood window replacements are also available, although the overall glass area is less than for vinyl replacements. Windows prices start at $225, and will cost $400 to $600 installed.

Window Replacement

Replacing the whole window—called *prime window replacement*—is required if your old frames are damaged beyond repair, if you want to enlarge the opening or if the style you want isn't available in a sash- or frame-replacement kit. It involves ripping out the entire assembly and installing a completely new window. It also requires installing new trim and cutting or repairing the exterior siding and interior walls.

This approach offers the largest selection of styles and materials. The windows vary widely in price; vinyl windows start at about $300, and wood windows at about $400 for a 3 × 5-ft. double-pane window.

SOURCES

Windows

ANDERSEN WINDOWS: 800/426-4261;
www.andersenwindows.com
CARADCO: 800/238-1866; www.caradco.com
CERTAINTEED: 800/782-8777; www.certainteed.com
CRESTLINE WINDOWS & DOORS: 715/693-7000;
www.crestline-online.com
EAGLE WINDOW & DOOR: 800/453-3633;
www.eaglewindow.com
HURD MILLWORK: 800/223-4873; www.hurd.com
KOLBE & KOLBE MILLWORK: 715/842-5666;
www.kolbe-kolbe.com
MARVIN WINDOWS & DOORS: 800/346-5128;
www.marvin.com
MILGARD WINDOWS: 800/645-4273; www.milgard.com
OWENS CORNING: 800/438-7465;
www.owenscorning.com
PEACHTREE DOORS & WINDOWS: 800/732-2499;
www.peach99.com
PELLA CORP.: 800/847-3552; www.pella.com
POZZI WOOD WINDOWS: 800/257-9663; www.pozzi.com
SIMONTON WINDOWS: 800/746-6686; www.simonton.com
VETTER WINDOWS: 800/838-8372;
www.vetterwindows.com
WEATHER SHIELD WINDOWS & DOORS: 800/477-6808;
www.weathershield.com
SILVERLINE WINDOWS: 800/234-4228;
www.silverlinewindows.com

Adding a Bay Window

Adding a bay window to your kitchen or eating area invites more light into the room and creates a new focal point for both the interior and exterior of your home. Bay windows reach out to capture sunlight and views and provide a sunny perch for reading or dining. They come in many styles, and the following tips can make it easier to choose the right one.

Selecting a Style

A bay window is simply three windows that are joined into a single unit. The wide center window is flanked by narrower casement or double-hung windows.

The two major styles of bay windows are distinguished by the angle of the two side panels. In the most common style, the side panels are slanted away from the wall, typically at a 30- or 45-degree angle. The other style, the box bay, is basically a square or rectangular box in which the side panels protrude straight out from the house at a 90-degree angle. A box bay with a glass roof is often referred to as a garden bay or greenhouse window.

Most bay windows are made of wood or vinyl—exterior finish options include wood, extruded vinyl and aluminum- or vinyl-clad wood. Wood windows are the most economical, but must be periodically repainted. Vinyl windows are affordable and maintenance-free, but their interior frames are also vinyl, which some people find less attractive. Clad wood windows usually cost more, but they offer both a low-maintenance vinyl or aluminum exterior and a handsome wood interior.

Most bays come with insulated double-glazing. For higher energy efficiency, choose a window with argon gas between the panes and a low-e coating.

Prices vary widely, so it's important to shop around to get the best style and price. A 3-ft.-high × 6-ft.-wide vinyl-clad 30-degree bay window will typically cost between $800 and $1,100. A custom-made unit will cost at least 15 to 20 percent more and take four to six weeks for delivery (compared with less than a week for a standard bay).

■ *Left: A bay window can be especially nice over the sink—where you spend most of your time in the kitchen.*

■ *Above: A box bay or greenhouse window can provide a sunny counter for your herbs or flowering plants.*

Installing it Properly

Before you buy a bay window, consider the following installation questions.

What size should I get?

It's easier and cheaper to install a bay that's the same size or smaller than the old window. A wider bay requires a larger opening and a new header, which can add $300 to $500 to the cost. On the other hand, a larger window does offer the advantages of bringing in more light and creating a greater visual impact, both inside and out.

What style should I get?

There's no set rule. A taller, narrower bay often looks better with a casement style, and a shorter unit tends to look better with a double-hung style. You can also match the style used on the other windows in your home. However, these are simply guidelines; pick the style that you like best. Although the center window of a bay is usually fixed, you can also order one with an operable casement or double-hung sash.

How will I support the window?

Most bay windows must be supported from below with braces or from above with steel cables bolted to the overhead framing. Both approaches work well, but support cables are less obtrusive because they're hidden inside the window frame. Not all manufacturers offer support cables, but they can be bought separately and adapted for use on almost any bay window.

Will the window fit under an eave?

Bay windows are often tucked beneath an eave. Before choosing a window, measure the horizontal depth of the eave, and try to get a unit that's shallow enough to fit beneath it. Most 30-degree bay windows are 12 to 14 in. deep; most 45-degree units are 16 to 22 in. deep; box bays and 60-degree bays are usually 18 to 24 in. deep.

What if there's no eave?

If there's no overhead eave above the window—or if your bay will stick out beyond the eave—you'll need an angled roof over the window to keep out the weather. In the past, these roofs had to be custom-cut by a specialist. Fortunately, prefabricated roof kits are now available for most bay windows. These reduce installation time

■ *The roof of this bay window and the skirt below it were made from kits and finished to blend with the home's exterior.*

and can be installed by any remodeling professional. Matching skirt kits for finishing the underside of the window are also available.

Who should install the window?

An experienced remodeler or carpenter should have no trouble installing a bay window, but it's not a job for everyone. The installation may require advanced skills—from modifying a load-bearing wall to patching exterior trim. Not to mention installing and supporting the window, which is likely to be large and very heavy. Considering the challenges of the job and the cost of the window, it's worth it to pay for a quality installation.

SOURCES

Bay Windows & Roof Kits

FLINTWOOD PRODUCTS (BAY WINDOW ROOF KITS): 800/728-4365; www.flintwood.com

ALL OF THE WINDOW MANUFACTURERS LISTED ON PAGE 141 OFFER BAY WINDOWS.

■ *Left: In most kitchens, one skylight is all
you need; it will provide plenty of light and
minimize heat gain and loss.*

most recommend between 5 and 15 percent of the floor area, and some even suggest less than 5 percent.

If your skylight is too large (or if you
install too many small ones), it will over-
heat the room during warm weather. Be
sure to keep the skylight ratio low if your
kitchen has lots of vertical windows; this
combination is especially prone to overheating. If the room has only a few other
windows, a larger skylight ratio might
make sense, as long as you use a glazing
with low solar heat gain.

Ensuring Comfort & Efficiency

Skylights aren't energy efficient; in summer they heat up the home quickly, and in
winter they can't collect heat because the
sun is too low in the sky. They're an easy
escape route for heated air, and the most
energy-efficient models can reduce light
transmission, which is the main reason for
buying a skylight in the first place.

To address these concerns, choose a skylight with good ratings (see page 140). In
a cold-winter climate, look for a window
that has a U-value of .45 or lower and that
lets in little solar heat but plenty of light.

A SHGC between .30 and .50 is best for
avoiding summer overheating, and a visible light rating
above .70 is optimal for light transmission.

Like windows, skylights come with energy-efficient
glazing options, such as low-e and tinted glass. Green
tints are better than bronze tints for reducing solar heat
gain while still letting in plenty of visible light.

You can find skylights anywhere you buy windows.
Most are packaged for shipping, which means you can't
inspect the one you're buying in the store. However, you
or your contractor should inspect the package on delivery. Make sure that all parts are in good condition, all
materials, including clips, flashing and screws, are provided and installation instructions are included. (Since
different manufacturers have different specs, even professionals need instructions.)

Skylights

A single skylight can transform a dark, closed-in kitchen
into a light, airy room bathed in warm, natural light—in
fact, a skylight can even be a kitchen's sole source of natural light. However, there are also many pitfalls to
adding a skylight to your kitchen, and careful planning
is necessary to get good results.

Sizing Skylights

It's a common mistake to overestimate the size or number of skylights your kitchen needs. In reality, a single
two-by-four-foot skylight (or a pair of two-by-two skylights) is just about right for a typical kitchen. Although
experts disagree about how much glass area is enough,

Skylight Options

Skylights are available in many shapes and sizes, including "solar tubes" that offer easy installation and reduced heat loss. Although most skylights are fixed and do not operate, others—sometimes called *roof windows*—can be opened and shut, and some have hidden ventilating systems. Wood and vinyl frames are both available, but both are typically covered with low-maintenance aluminum, so there's little difference between them in price or performance.

Glazing

Building codes require that skylights have either tempered or laminated glass. Both stand up to snow loads and protect against falling objects. Tempered glass breaks into small pieces if damaged. Laminated glass, which is fused with a thin layer of plastic, stays in place if broken. It's also better at keeping out sound and is more energy efficient, although also more expensive. Many skylights compromise, offering an outside pane of tempered glass and an inside pane of laminated glass.

Skylights are also available with plastic glazing. Although this is less energy efficient than glass, it costs less and can be formed into domes and curved shapes.

Condensation Channel

During the winter, moist air inside your home tends to collect and condense on the underside of a skylight. On older models, this condensation often drips back into the living area, where it's mistaken for a leak. Newer models have a channel that collects condensation and allows it to evaporate without dripping.

■ *Above: The light, airy feeling of this kitchen corner is the result of a clever arrangement of windows and skylights.*

Flashing

Skylights are vulnerable to leaks from the outside—in fact, this is the biggest complaint about older models. Good-quality skylights now come with flashing systems that are customized for specific applications. On a flat roof, a skylight must be attached to a wood curb that raises it 4 to 6 in. above the roof deck.

Operating Tools

If your skylight is operable, you'll most likely need a tool or attachment that enables you to reach up and open and close the window. Although a long pole is the usual method, there are also motorized versions that are operated by remote controls or wall switches. However, these handy automated features can easily double the cost of your skylight.

SOURCES

Skylights

ANDERSEN WINDOWS: 800/426-4261; www.andersenwindows.com
CRESTLINE WINDOWS & DOORS: 715/693-7000; www.crestline-online.com
FISHER SKYLIGHTS: 800/368-7732; www.fisherskylights.com
NATURALITE: 800/527-4018; www.vistawall.com
PELLA: 800/847-3552; www.pella.com
SOLATUBE: 800/966-7652; www.solarcb.com
VELUX: 800/688-3589; www.velux.com
WEATHER SHIELD WINDOWS & DOORS: 800/477-6808; www.weathershield.com
WASCO PRODUCTS: 800/388-0293; www.wascoproducts.com

Worksheet 1: Assessing Your Needs

Use this questionnaire to record the kitchen elements you want to change during your remodeling project. Refer to Chapter 2 for more information.

Layout & Floor Plan

1. The floor plan and the arrangement of elements are adequate in my kitchen; all I need is a simple **cosmetic makeover____**.

2. My kitchen is big enough, but I'd like to **rearrange the layout** to redirect traffic and create a more efficient space____.

3. My kitchen is spacious enough, but the traffic patterns are a nuisance. I want to move doors and windows to **redirect traffic** and improve efficiency____.

4. My kitchen is too small; I need to expand by **moving interior walls____**.

5. My kitchen is too small; I'm pulling out all the stops by **adding a room addition** to my kitchen____.

6. I need a **new/larger eating area** in my kitchen____.

7. I'd like to **add an island** to my kitchen. I'll be using it for a sink____, cooktop____, eating counter____.

8. I could really make use of a **home office center** in my kitchen____.

Appliances & Fixtures

9. My appliances work adequately, but I'm tired of them. Maybe I can **repaint or reface the appliances____**.

10. I need to install a **new cooktop/range____, wall oven____, vent hood____**.

11. I need a **new refrigerator,** a built-in____, slide-in____.

12. I'd like to buy some **new small appliances**, including: microwave____, food disposer____, dishwasher____, trash compactor____.

13. My sink has seen better days; time to install a **new sink–** single-____, double-____, triple-____bowl.

14. I'd like to **add a second sink** to my kitchen____.

15. I want some **fun stuff**, like a **built-in stereo____** or an **under-cabinet television set____**.

Storage

16. Though they provide adequate storage, my **cabinets need to be painted or refinished____**.

17. I want to **add storage accessories** to my present cabinets including: slide-out drawers____, pantry shelves____, lazy Susan corner shelves____.

18. My present cabinets aren't bad, but to expand my storage, I need to **add more cabinets____**.

19. I loathe my cabinets for various reasons; time to **replace the cabinets** altogether____.

Work areas

20. My countertops are ugly or in bad shape; I want to **install new countertops,** and I prefer: laminate ____, ceramic tile____, solid-surface____, (other) ____.

21. I need **more countertop space** around my: cooktop____, wall oven____, refrigerator____, sink____.

22. I need a **larger primary meal preparation area** (36" minimum) ____.

Power & Lighting

23. Because I often blow fuses or trip circuit breakers, I need to **install more electrical circuits____**.

24. I need to **add more outlets** for plug-in appliances____.

25. I need to **add dedicated 240-volt circuits** for my electric range/cooktop____, wall oven____.

26. I'll **add____ dedicated 120-volt circuits** for the microwave, dishwasher, food disposer, trash compactor.

27. I need to **increase overall lighting** by installing: overhead lights____, windows____, a skylight____.

28. The work areas in my kitchen are badly illuminated; I need to **add task lights____**.

29. I'd like to **add decorative lighting** to my kitchen____.

30. My kitchen could really use a **telephone outlet____** or **cable TV jack____**.

Floors, Walls & Ceilings

31. My floor surfaces are pretty solid. Maybe all I need to do is **refinish the hardwood floors____**.

32. My present flooring is really ugly or worn; no choice but to **install new flooring**. I'm leaning toward: vinyl flooring____, ceramic tile____, laminate flooring____, solid-wood flooring____, (other)____.

33. For a **decorative wall finish**, I'm choosing: paint____, wallpaper____, ceramic tile____, wood paneling____, mirrors____, decorative moldings____.

34. My **ceiling finish** will be painted____, lightly textured____, or covered with decorative metal panels____.

Worksheet 2: Create Your Drawings

Use the icons shown here and ¼-in. graph paper to create drawings for your new kitchen. Use a scale of ½ in.= 1 ft. (1 square = 6 in.) when drawing your plans; the icons are drawn to match this scale.

Plan view (overhead) templates for 24-in.-deep base cabinets

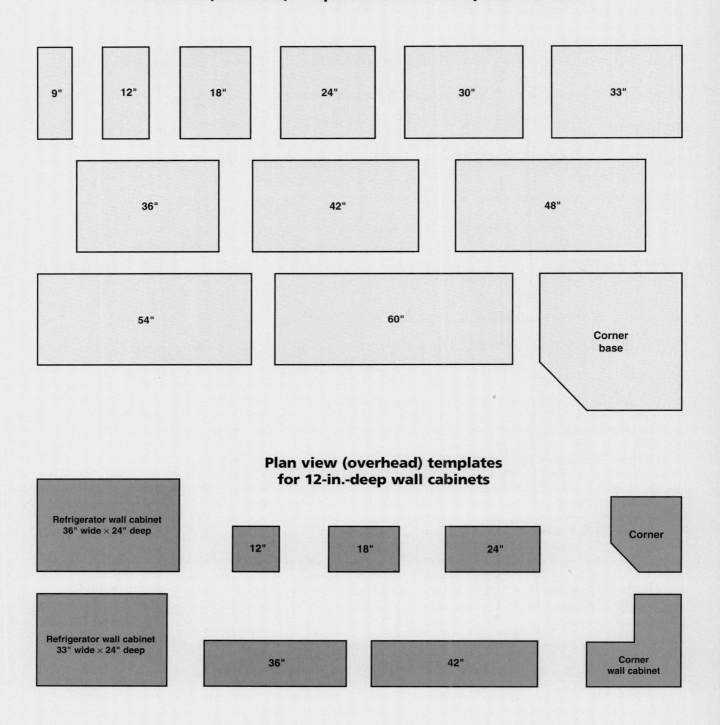

Plan view (overhead) templates for 12-in.-deep wall cabinets

Basic construction symbols (not to scale)

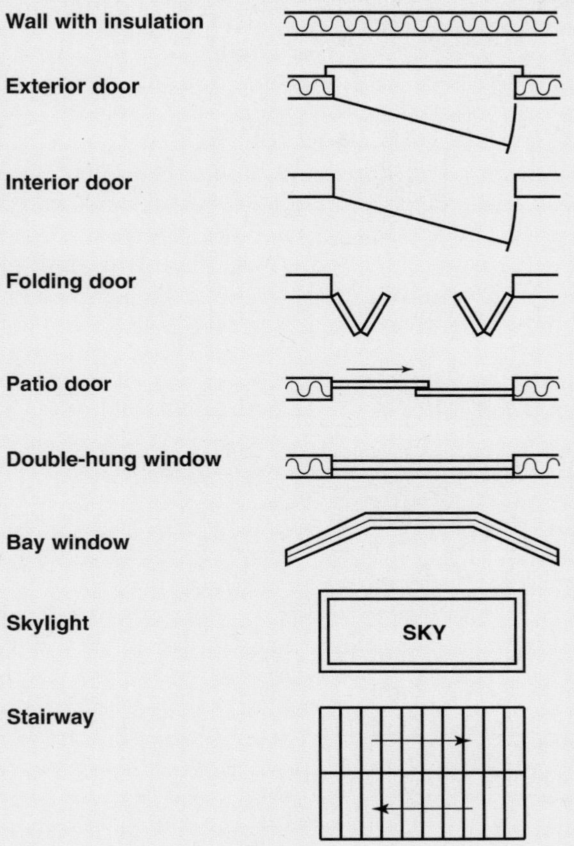

Wall with insulation

Exterior door

Interior door

Folding door

Patio door

Double-hung window

Bay window

Skylight

SKY

Stairway

Range/cooktop, 30" wide

WO

Oven, 27" wide

DW

Dishwasher, 24" wide

R

Refrigerator, 32" wide

Electrical symbols

120-volt GFCI outlet — GFCI

Range outlet — R

Single-pole switch S

Three-way switch S₃

Vent fan F

Thermostat T

Telephone outlet

Incandescent ceiling fixture

Wall-mounted light fixture

Recessed light fixture R

Fluorescent light fixture

Track light fixture

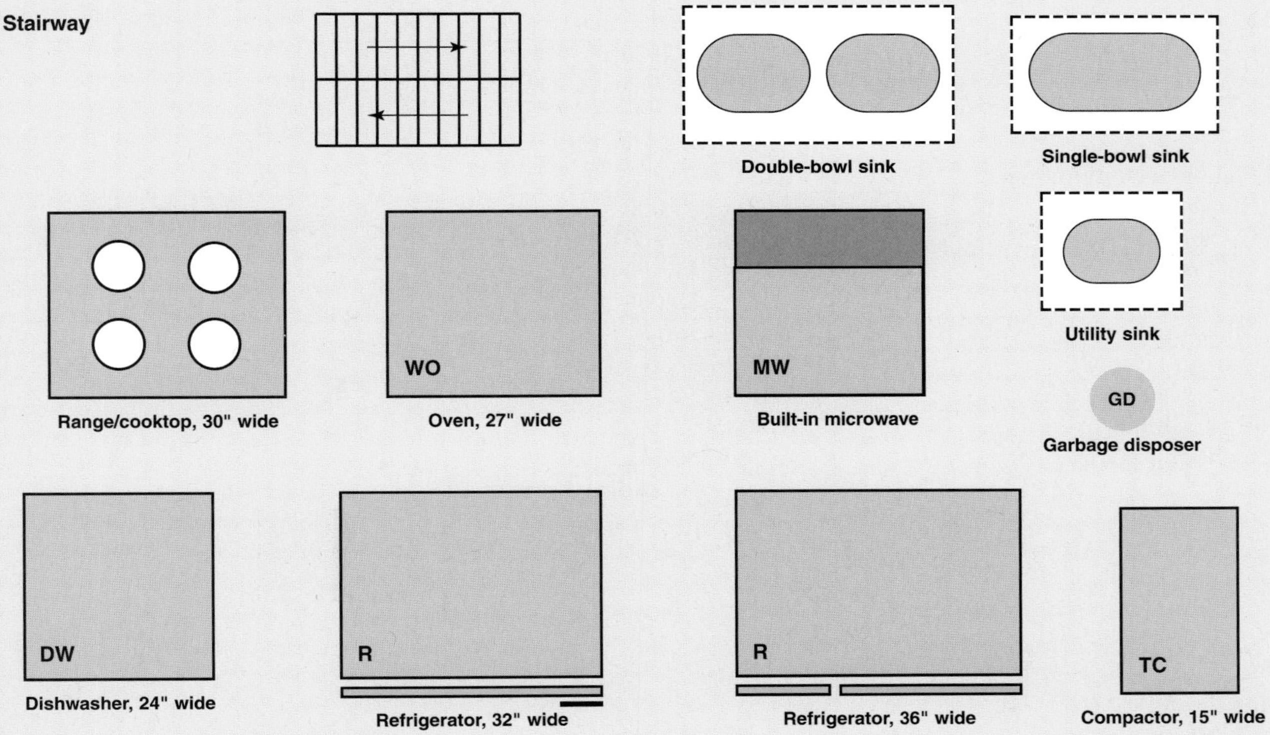

Double-bowl sink

Single-bowl sink

MW

Built-in microwave

Utility sink

GD

Garbage disposer

R

Refrigerator, 36" wide

TC

Compactor, 15" wide

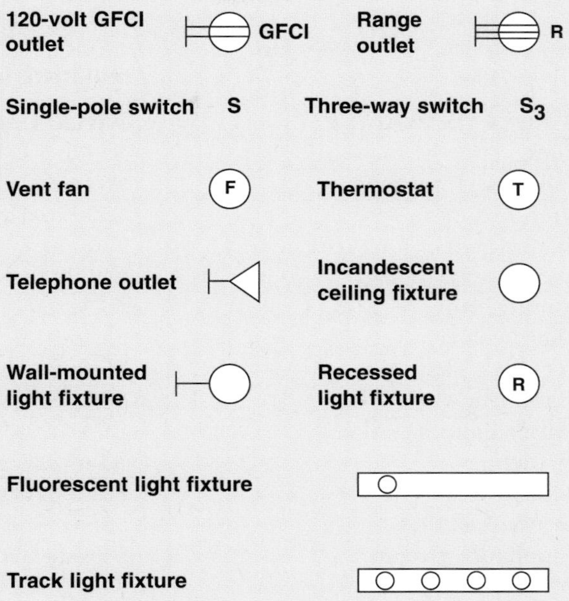

Worksheet 3: Estimating Your Budget

Budget Goal: $_____

KITCHEN ELEMENT	ESTIMATED PRICE RANGE	MY BUDGET
Construction of room addition	$70 to $120/sq. ft.	
Walls, rough framing	$3 to $5/sq. ft.	
Exterior doors	$300 to $1,200	
Interior doors	$100 to $350	
Patio doors	$1,000 to $2,500	
Flooring, vinyl	$3 to $15/sq. ft.	
hardwood	$5 to $15/sq. ft.	
ceramic tile	$5 to $30/sq. ft.	
laminate	$8 to $20/sq. ft.	
Wall/ceiling, drywall	$.75 to $3/sq. ft.	
paneling	$3 to $20/sq. ft.	
ceramic tile	$5 to $20/sq. ft.	
Electrical, outlets	$35 to $80	
appliance circuit	$150 to $200	
electric baseboard heat	$40 to $50/lin. ft.	
Walls, paint	$.06 to $.15/sq. ft.	
wallpaper	$1 to $5/sq. ft.	
Cabinets & trim	$100 to $350/lin. ft.	
Countertops, laminate	$20 to $50/lin. ft.	
ceramic tile	$5 to $30/sq. ft.	
solid–surface	$100 to $150/lin. ft.	
stainless steel	$70 to $140/lin. ft.	
natural stone	$150 to $450/lin. ft.	
Sink (faucet, plumbing)	$300 to $700	
Range	$400 to $3,000	
Cooktop	$200 to $1,200	
Wall oven	$250 to $1,000	
Refrigerator	$600 to $3,000	
Microwave	$200 to $600	
Garbage disposer	$150 to $300	
Dishwasher	$300 to $700	
Trash compactor	$150 to $350	
Lighting fixtures	$30 to $300 ea.	
	Total Estimate:	

Worksheet 4: Loan Application Information

When you apply for a home improvement or equity loan, the officer
of the financial institution may need the following information:

Name of Applicant: _____ Social Security Number: _____

Address: _____

City: _____ State: _____

Telephone: _____

Employer: _____

Position: _____ Years employed: _____ Monthly income: _____

Co-signer: _____ Social Security Number: _____

Employer: _____

Position: _____ Years employed: _____ Monthly income: _____

Savings Account: Bank _____ Account # _____

Checking Account: Bank _____ Account # _____

Home Mortgage: Lender _____ Account # _____

Auto Loan: Lender _____ Account # _____ Balance _____

Credit Cards: _____ Account # _____ Balance _____

_____ Account # _____ Balance _____

_____ Account # _____ Balance _____

_____ Account # _____ Balance _____

Other Debts: _____

_____

Other Assets: _____

_____

Loan Amount Sought: _____ Payback Preference (yrs): _____

Worksheet 5: Sample of Independent Contractor Agreement

Independent Contractor Agreement

This Agreement is made on _____, 20_____,

between_____, Owner,

residing at_____, City of_____, State of _____,

and _____, Contractor,

residing at_____, City of_____, State of _____ .

For valuable consideration, the Owner and Contractor agree as follows:

1. The Contractor agrees to furnish all the labor and materials to do the following work for the Owner as an independent contractor:

2. The Contractor agrees that the following portions of the total work will be completed by the dates specified:

   WORK   DATE

3. The Contractor agrees to perform this work in a professional manner according to standard practices. If any plans or specifications are part of this job, they are attached to and are part of the contract.

4. The Owner agrees to pay the Contractor as full payment $ _____, for doing the work outlined above. This price will be paid to the Contractor on satisfactory completion of the work in the following manner and on the following dates:

5. The Contractor is adequately insured for injury to his or her employees and the injury of others as a result of acts of the Contractor, his or her employees, and the employees of any subcontractors.

6. The Contractor and Owner may agree to extra services and work, but any such change orders must be set out and agreed to in writing by both the Contractor and the Owner.

7. The Contractor will obtain all permits necessary for the work to be performed.

8. The Contractor agrees to remove all debris and leave the premises in broom-clean condition.

9. The Contractor agrees to indemnify and hold the Owner harmless from any claims or liability arising from the Contractor's work under this Contract.

10. The Contractor warrants all work for a period of _____ months following completion of the work.

11. All disputes shall be resolved by binding arbitration in accordance with the rules of the American Arbitration Association.

12. No modification of this Contract will be effective unless it is in writing and is signed by both parties. This Contract binds and benefits both parties and any successors. Time is of the essence in this contract. This document, including any attachments, is the entire agreement between the parties. This Contract is governed by the laws of the State of _____.

Dated:_____, witnessed by_____

_____
(Signature of Owner)

_____
(Printed name of Owner)

_____
(Signature of Contractor)

_____
(Printed name of Contractor)

Worksheet 6: Sample of Standard Lien Release Document

RELEASE OF MECHANIC'S LIEN

The following contractor has furnished materials, labor, or both for work at the property owned by _____,
located at _____, City of _____, State of _____.

_____, _____, _____, _____
(contractor)   (address)   (city)   (state/zip)

This contractor hereby releases all liens and the right to file any lien against this property for materials or labor provided as of this date. This release does not, however, constitute a release of any sums which may be due to this contractor for materials or labor.

The parties signing this release intend that it both bind and benefit themselves and any successors.

Dated _____

_____
(contractor signature)

State of _____

County of _____
On_____, _____ personally came before me and, being duly sworn, did state that he/she is the person described in the above document and that he/she signed the above document in my presence.

_____
(Notary signature)

Notary Public, for the County of _____
State of _____
My commission expires_____   Seal

Resources:

American Institute of Architects
(202) 626-7300
(800) 364-9364
www.aiaonline.com

American Society of Interior Designers
608 Massachusetts Ave., NE
Washington, DC 20002-6006
(202) 546-3480
www.asid.org

Association of Home Appliance Manufacturers
Suite 402
1111 19th St., NW
Washington, DC 20036
(202) 872-5955
www.aham.org

Council of Better Business Bureaus
4200 Wilson Blvd.
Suite 8000
Arlington, VA 22203-1838
(703) 276-0100
www.bbb.org

U.S. Dept of Housing & Urban Development (HUD)
www.hud.gov

Improvenet (home improvement and loan information)
www.improvenet.com

Internal Revenue Service
www.irs.ustreas.gov/prod/

National Association of the Remodeling Industry (NARI)
4900 Seminary Rd.
Suite 320
Alexandria, VA 22311
(703) 575-1100
www.nari.org

National Kitchen & Bath Association (NKBA)
687 Willow Grove St.
Hackettstown, NJ 07840
(800) 843-6522
www.nkba.com

National Wood Flooring Association
16388 Westwoods Business Park
Ellisville, MO 63021
(800) 422-4556
www.woodfloors.org

Tile Council of America
100 Clemson Research Blvd.
Anderson, SC 29625
(864) 646-8453
www.tileusa.com

United Homeowners Association
(202) 408-8842
www.uha.org

Additional Reading from Creative Publishing international:

Carpentry: Remodeling
Carpentry: Tools, Shelves, Walls, Doors
Complete Guide to Home Plumbing
Complete Guide to Home Wiring
Complete Guide to Painting & Decorating
Flooring Projects & Techniques
Refinishing & Finishing Wood
Remodeling Kitchens

Contributors:

Note: T=Top, C=Center, B=Bottom, L=Left, R=Right, I=Inset

Aristokraft, Inc.: pp. 39, 44
One Aristokraft Square
P. O. Box 420
Jasper, IN 47546
tel: 812-482-2527
fax: 812-482-1763
www.aristokraft.com

Armstrong Residential Floors:
p. 122
600 Third Ave., sixth floor
New York, NY 10016
tel: 800-233-3823
fax: 212-697-2646
www.armstrongfloors.com

Bruce Hardwood Floors: p. 128
16803 Dallas Parkway
Addison, TX 75001
tel: 214-887-2361
fax: 214-887-2234
www.brucelaminatefloors.com

Delta Faucet Company:
pp. 35L, 97B
55 East 111th Street
Indianapolis, IN 46280
tel: 317-848-1812
fax: 317-571-6508
www.deltafaucet.com

GE Appliances:
pp. 103, 104, 105, 109T, 111
Appliance Park
Louisville, KY 40225
tel: 502-452-5619
fax: 502-452-0471
www.ge.com/appliances

Kolbe & Kolbe Millwork Co. Inc.:
p. 153
1323 S. Eleventh Avenue
Wausau, WI 55401
tel: 715-842-5666
fax: 715-845-8270
www.kolbe-kolbe.com

KraftMaid Cabinetry:
pp. 28, 29, 110
P. O. Box 1055
Middlefield, OH 44062
tel: 800-571-1990
fax: 440-632-5648
www.kraftmaid.com

Laufen Ceramic Tile: p. 93
6531 North Laufen Drive
Tulsa, OK 74117
tel: 800-331-3651
fax: 918-428-0695
www.usa.laufen.com

Italian Trade Commission-New York: Ceramic Tile Department:
p. 125L
499 Park Ave
New York, NY 10022
Fax: 212-758-1050

Marvin Windows and Doors:
p. 57 R
P. O. Box 100
Warroad, MN 56763
tel: 888-537-8268
fax: 651-452-3074
www.marvin.com

Pergo Inc.: pp. 15, 127
3128 Highwoods Blvd.
Raleigh, NC 27604
tel: 919-773-6000
Fax: 919-773-5123
www.pergo.com

Progress Lighting: p. 57L
101 Corporate Drive
Spartanberg, SC 29303-5007
tel: 864-599-6000
fax: 864-599-6151
www.progresslighting.com

Sonoma Tilemakers: p. 45T
7750 Bell Road
Windsor, CA 95492
tel: 707-837-8177
fax: 707-837-9472
www.sonomatilemakers.com

Snaidero U.S.A. Design:
pp. 33B, 89T
201 West 132nd Street
Los Angeles, CA 90061
tel: 310-516-8499
fax: 310-516-9918
www.snaidero.com

Sub-Zero Freezer Company, Inc.:
pp. 108, 109B
P. O. Box 44130
Madison, WI 53744-4130
tel: 800-222-7820
fax: 608-270-3339
www.subzero.com

Wilsonart International, Inc.:
pp. 41, 50, 54, 56 both,
91, 120, 126
240 Wilson Place
Temple, TX 76504
tel: 800-443-3222
fax: 254-207-2384
www.wilsonart.com

Wood-Mode, Inc.:
pp. 12B, 89B
One Second Street
Kreamer, PA 17833
tel: 570-374-2711
fax: 570-372-1422
www.wood-mode.com

Photography Credits:

Susan Andrews
Interior Avenues
Overland Park, KS
©Roy Inman: p. 30

Bob Firth
Firth Photobank
Shakopee, MN
©Bob Firth: p. 11T

Andy Freeberg
Mill Valley, CA
©Andy Freeberg: p. 27B

Nancy Hill
Ridgefield, CT
©Nancy Hill for the
following designers:
Kitchens By Deane: pp. 21, 32, 40;
Margie Little: p. 25B; Cornerstone
Ltd.: p. 102; Kitchen Design
Studio: p. 107

Robert Kern
Fair Lawn, NJ
©Robert Kern: p. 25L
©Robert Kern for the
following designers:
Ulrich, Inc.: p. 58; Bothzeid,
Kaiserman, Thompson & Bee:
p. 119

David Livingston
Mill Valley, CA
©www.davidduncanlivingston.com:
front cover, back cover both,
pp. 17L, 20B, 26 both, 31, 48, 70,
85, 88, 94B, 96, 97T, 99 both, 101,
123, 125B, 130, 131, 134, 138,
142L

Lisa Masson
Annapolis, MD
©Lisa Masson: pp. 13, 84, 133L,
141, 145

Joshua McHugh
New York, NY
©Joshua McHugh: p. 19B

Karen Melvin
Architectural Stock Images, Inc.
Minneapolis, MN
©Karen Melvin: p. 90
©Karen Melvin for the
following designers:
Andersen Windows Corporation:
pp. 12T, 116; Sandra Mangel,
ASID: p. 19; Lecy Construction:
p. 35R; Jean Larson, AIA, SALA
Architects: p. 91; Knapp Cabinetry
& Woodworking: pp. 86, 94T; Rick
Lundin, AIA, Construct
Architects: p. 112; Geoffrey
Warner: p. 114; Lynn Monson,
Monson Interior Design: p. 115;
Jone Mosher, Allied Member
ASID, Gabberts Interior Design:
p. 117; McNulty Homes: p. 129;
Kathy Koutsky, Portobello Design:
p. 142R; Kolbe & Kolbe Millwork:
p. 143

Melabee M. Miller
Hillside, NJ
©Melabee M. Miller: p. 17R
©Melabee M. Miller for the
following designers:
Richard and Linda Kregloski:
p. 11B; Steve Meltzer, Abbey's
Kitchens Baths & Interiors: p. 16;
Jennifer Pacca, Award Interiors:
p. 20L; Geraldine Kaupp Interiors:
p. 36 both; Lawrence-Mayer
Interiors: p. 140

Robert Perron
Branford, CT
©Robert Perron: pp. 14, 23

Holly Stickley
Tigard, OR
©Holly Stickley for the
following designers:
Greg Heinze-Sandy Hume:
pp. 101, 132, 133R; Nicole
Raate-Barbara Martin: p. 92;
Pat Killen, AIA: p. 95;
William Hefner, AIA: p. 124;
Vikki O'Leal, ASID: p. 136

Roger Turk
Northlight Photography, Inc.
Southworth, WA
©Roger Turk: pp. 9, 10, 18, 24,
27T, 33, 34, 38, 45B, 106, 118, 144

Jessie Walker
Glencoe, IL
©Jessie Walker: pp. 8, 22, 137

Illustration Credits:

**©Trevor Johnston &
Paul Perrault:**
p. 139

Index: